CONTENTS

1)	Introduction to Owen Wister	1
2)	Introduction to The Virginian	11
3)	Textual Analysis	
	Chapters 1–6	41
	Chapter 7–12	50
	Chapters 18–22	63
	Chapters 23–25	67
	Chapters 26–29	71
	Chapters 30–33	76
	Chapters 34–36	81
4)	Character Analyses	84
5)	Commentary	90
6)	Survey of Criticism	95
7)	Essay Questions and Answers	98
8)	Bibliography	102

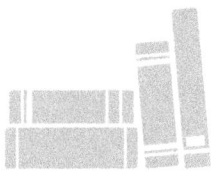

INTRODUCTION TO OWEN WISTER

TO THE READER

The reader of *The Virginian* will find the novel familiar in several ways. Its author has often been called "the father of the Western" because the book contains many scenes and situations which appeared first in this novel and which have become a standard part of the myth of the great American West during the post-Civil-War period. Not the least of these elements are the personal characteristics of the novel's hero, who is known to us only as "the Virginian." Unlike many of his predecessors in Western fiction, he is portrayed as a man to whom courage, loyalty, common sense, justice, chivalry, humor and morality are the ingredients of the good life. While it may seem like a somewhat naive plot when compared to many contemporary works which achieve the antithesis of virtue under the guise of "sophistication" or *realism*, *The Virginian* is an example of the popularity of the *theme* in which good triumphs over evil and the hero wins the girl. This plot has sufficed for heroes as old as those in the Bible and as new as James Bond.

The Virginian sold over a million copies in its first six years of publication; today that number is nearing the four million mark. Allowing for the sentimentality and gentility common to the age in which it was written, its success is a remarkable record. The story has also been adapted for the stage, three movie versions and a television series. It is available in several paperback editions and has been translated into several foreign languages. In this outline we will examine through plot and character analysis and commentary several of the factors which have made the novel an American classic since its publication in 1902.

BIOGRAPHICAL BACKGROUND

Owen Wister was born in Philadelphia, Pennsylvania on July 14, 1860. His paternal antecedents had come to Philadelphia in the early 1700s and prospered as merchants. Wister's father, Dr. Owen Jones Wister, had served in the United States Navy for several years and sailed around the world in 1853. The boy's mother, Sarah Butler Wister, was the daughter of Fanny Kemble (1809–1893), a well-known Shakespearean actress and Pierce Butler, an affluent country gentleman from Georgia. The Butlers settled on a farm several miles from the center of Philadelphia. Called the "Butler Place," the property was transformed by Fanny Kemble Butler so that it resembled an English estate. Owen Wister spent his youth here and many years later occupied the home with his own wife and six children.

The family was well-to-do, socially prominent and culturally oriented. All of the Kembles had been famous artists, either on the stage or in the field of music. Fanny Kemble had met Sir Walter Scott, corresponded with William Makepeace Thackeray and Robert Browning, visited and traveled in the leading intellectual and cultural circles of Europe and America. In Boston she became friends with the historians Dr. Channing, William Prescott, John Motley and the famous American writers,

Ralph Waldo Emerson, Oliver Wendell Holmes, James Russell Lowell and Henry Wadsworth Long-fellow. She also knew the composers Mendelssohn, von Weber and Liszt. She gave her grandson a letter of introduction to Liszt when Owen went to Europe to study music.

Owen Wister's mother inherited many of Fanny Kemble's tastes and talents. She spoke French and Italian, translated poetry, contributed to the *Atlantic Monthly*, was an adept musician, and continued to make Butler Place a center of intellectual and cultural activity. Owen Wister was twelve when Henry James, an old friend of Fanny Kemble's first stayed at Butler Place. Many details of what life there was like during Wister's childhood can be found in Fanny Kemble's *Records of A Girlhood* (1879) and *Records of Later Life* (1882).

EARLY EDUCATION

At the age of six Owen Wister attended a boarding school in Switzerland for three months while his parents traveled in Europe. Four years later he spent a year in school at Hofwyl, Switzerland while his parents visited Fanny Kemble, who had returned to live in England. The following year, 1871, he lived with relatives in England and attended a public school there. Returning to Philadelphia, Wister attended Germantown Academy for a year and in 1873 went off to boarding school at St. Paul's School, Concord, New Hampshire. At St. Paul's Wister advanced quickly in the two talents of his life - music and writing. He wrote stories and articles for the school paper and eventually became an editor; he also published poetry and was active in the choir. In 1878 Wister graduated from St. Paul's and he entered Harvard University the following fall.

COLLEGE LIFE

At Harvard, Wister subordinated his interest in writing and majored in music. He wrote the words and music for a Hasty Pudding Club production entitled "Dido and Aeneas". Wister was elected to Phi Beta Kappa and graduated with honors in 1882. The same year he published his first novel, a **burlesque** of *Swiss Family Robinson*. Wister formed many lasting friendships in college. Perhaps the most famous was with Theodore Roosevelt. A few of his other close friends, some of whom were older than he, were Henry Higginson who founded the Boston Symphony, William Dean Howells, the writer and critic, and Oliver Wendell Holmes, Sr., the author, and Oliver Wendell Holmes, Jr., a future Associate Justice of the Supreme Court.

TWO OF A KIND

The relationship of Wister and Theodore Roosevelt is told in Wister's biography of his friend, Roosevelt, *The Story of a Friendship* (1930). The two men shared not only many college experiences but also the common experience of overcoming poor health, a common love of the great West and many similar views of life. *The Virginian* is dedicated to Teddy Roosevelt with the following inscription:

> **Some of these pages you have seen, some you have praised, one stands new-written because you blamed it; and all, my dear critic, beg leave to remind you of their author's changeless admiration.**

The pages which Roosevelt had seen and praised were short stories which later became part of the novel. Those pages "blamed" included a realistic scene having to do with the bloody gouging of a horse's eye. The original account, in fact one based on a true incident, can be read in Wister's journal, but there is little doubt that it was Roosevelt's influence which gives us Chapter XXVI as it is. The chapter, entitled "Balaam and Pedro" had appeared with the original incident when it was published as a short story in Harper's Magazine eight years before the publication of the novel. Obviously it had taken several years of friendly argument before Wister yielded to his friend's suggestion. In later years Wister and his family visited the Roosevelts both at the White House and at the Roosevelt home at Oyster Bay, New York. Both Roosevelt and Wister tried to warn their countrymen to prepare for World War I shortly before America entered that conflict.

TRAVEL AND STUDY IN EUROPE

Desiring to become a composer, Wister decided to study music for a year under Ernest Guiraud at the Paris Conservatoire. But first he went on a Grand Tour with several college friends during the summer of 1882. In August he presented a letter of introduction to Franz Liszt from his grandmother. After listening to his music, Liszt felt he was a promising artist. At the end of the year's study, when Wister returned to America at his father's request, his teacher, Professor Guiraud echoed Liszt's remarks. However, it was destined that Wister would become known to the world for his literary endeavors rather than for his musical talent which it seems would have been an equal avenue to fame. His interest in music persisted throughout his life.

LEGAL INTERLUDE

Returning to the United States, Wister worked as a bank clerk in Boston. He became a member of the Tavern Club, which was destined to become a famous literary club, and wrote a novel with his cousin. On the advice of his friend, the well known writer, William Dean Howells, Wister did not attempt to publish the work. In 1885, Wister experienced some ill-health and his doctor advised him to spend the summer in the West. Wister spent the summer with friends in Wyoming. Although his health improved and he returned to Harvard Law School that fall, Wister's first summer in the West is noteworthy chiefly because it inspired his career as a writer. He graduated from law school in 1888, became associated with the Philadelphia law firm of Robert Ralston and Francis Rawle and was admitted to the bar in 1890. But a legal career, like a musical one, was unable to deter Wister from pursuing a writing career.

WESTERN TRAVELS

Between 1885 and 1900 Wister made a dozen trips to the West; he not only traveled to Wyoming but on to the Pacific, as far north as British Columbia and as far south as New Mexico and Texas. During these journeys he carefully kept journals which were unknown until recently. Today, the original journals are located in the Owen Wister Collection at the University of Wyoming Library. An excellent book containing the essence of the journals as well as other important biographical material was edited by Wister's daughter, Fanny Kemble Wister and published in 1958.

WRITER OF WESTERNS

Inspired by an enthusiastic dinner companion who shared his views of the West, Wister wrote his first Western story on an autumn night in 1891. Entitled "Hank's Women," it was accepted by Harper's Magazine. In January, 1892, Wister sold his second story, "How Lin Mc-Lean Went East," and by the spring of 1893, Wister was traveling in the West, writing articles and stories on assignment from Harper's. Red Men and White, Wister's first book of Western stories was published in 1895. Between trips to the West year after year Wister found time to visit Rudyard Kipling when the well known English writer was living in Vermont, and Henry James in England. In addition, Wister kept up his close acquaintance with a large circle of friends.

In 1898 Wister married a distant cousin, Mary Channing Wister. During the next fifteen years, Wister published a dozen books. He did not always limit himself to a Western setting nor only to the **genre** of the novel, but he did become a celebrity with the publication of *The Virginian* in 1902. Wister's married life was immensely happy and rewarding. He continued his lifelong habit of traveling widely but now he was accompanied by his wife and sometimes a few or all of their six children, three boys and three girls. After fifteen years of marriage, Mary Wister succumbed in childbirth. Wister never married again.

WORLD WAR AND AFTER

Wister's writing during the next few years took the form of essays in which he attempted to improve American relations with England and France and to warn his country against Germany. Following the Armistice, Wister fell into the habit of spending part of nearly every year in Europe. In England, he formed friendships with Lord Dunsany, Joseph Conrad and E. F. Benson. However, he did write two interesting works in his later years: *When West Was West* (1928) and Roosevelt, the *Story of a Friendship*. The latter book has already been mentioned and the former might have been called "the West revisited."

On July 21, 1938, Owen Wister died of a cerebral hemorrhage at the age of seventy-eight. Biographically, Wister clearly belongs to the genteel and Victorian movements of the last century rather than to the rebellious countermovements of our own.

"Evolution of the Cowpuncher": In an article entitled "The Evolution of the Cowpuncher" published in Harper's Magazine in 1895, Wister compares the cowpuncher of the American West, whom he observed at first hand during his many Western travels, to the knights of the days of old. A few excerpts will show Wister's fanciful analogy:

> From the tournament to the round-up! Deprive the Saxon of his horse, and put him to forest-clearing or in a countinghouse for a couple of generations and you may pass him by without ever seeing that his legs are designed for the gripping of saddles... So upon land has the horse been his foster brother, his ally, his playfellow, from the tournament of Camelot to the roundup at Abilene... Seventy-five dollars a month and absolute health and strength were his wages; and when the news of all this excellence drifted from Texas eastward, they came in shoals... Every sort and degree of home tradition came with them from their far birthplaces. Some had knelt in the family prayers at one time, others could remember no parent or teacher except the street; some spoke with the gentle accent of Virginia, others in the dialect of baked beans and codfish; here and there was the baccalaureate, already beginning to forget his Greek Alphabet.... No soldier of fortune ever adventured with bolder carelessness, no fiercer blood ever stained a border. War they made in plenty, but not

love; for the woman they saw was not the woman a man can take into his heart.

THE COWBOY - ROMANTIC HERO

The fact that much of the above passage is a highly romantic view of reality is obvious. It is interesting for several reasons. First, as a writer of popular magazine articles, Wister had to write, within certain limits, what the reading public wanted to read. America was ripe for a romantic Western hero and what better analogy could there be than to King Arthur and his Knights of the Round Table. Because of Alfred Lord Tennyson's *Idylls of the King*, the tales of knighthood were well known in America and England. A stock plot in these tales is that of the brave knight surviving some dire trial of combat and winning the hand of the fair princess. Perhaps the concluding line of the above passage explains why Wister imported Molly Stark Wood, the heroine of *The Virginian*, from the East. As the reader will discover, Molly is a girl whom a man can easily "take into his heart."

THE WIDE OPEN SPACES

Another aspect of the passage which reflects an interesting characteristic of the American culture is Wister's treatment of the countinghouse clerk who has forgotten, it seems, the glory of the open ranges and the vastness of the land. For Wister, the West held the same magnetism which the sea held for Herman Melville. The idea that the industrial revolution and urbanization tend to restrict the freedom of the human spirit has been a familiar one in American life and literature. Nathaniel Hawthorne described his painful experience at being penned up in a clerical position in the introductory chapter to

The Scarlet Letter. Ralph Waldo Emerson urged his countrymen to appreciate nature and develop self-reliance in many of his essays. Henry David Thoreau also preached the sermon of nature in Walden. Such popular poems as Stephen Vincent Benet's "The **Ballad** of William Sycamore" and Robert Frost's "Birches", "Stopping By the Woods on a Snowy Evening" and "After Apple Picking" also seem to lament the countryside which yields to super highways, shopping centers and cities.

As can be seen in the domestic issues of our own day, the problem of the proper balance between urban and rural development, industrial and recreational lands, clean and polluted waters, roadside landscaping and billboard advertising is still with us. While Theodore Roosevelt, to whom conservation and natural beauty were of prime importance and Owen Wister, to whom the frontier presented an image of heroic American Lancelots could never imagine a time when even the air we breathe would need to be carefully protected against pollution, they both recognized that the West they loved was a quickly "vanishing world". Both men were realistic enough to know that they could not halt the progress of the young and dynamic republic, but both did their country a service; Wister, by catching this brief period of its history in the spirit of *The Virginian,* and Roosevelt by using his great office to urge his fellow citizens to set aside great parcels of land to be preserved for all time, so that future generations might relive the days of their forebears in a virgin and natural environment. It is directly due to the efforts of Teddy Roosevelt that the people of the United States, through the efforts of their government, are still the largest single owner of national forest lands.

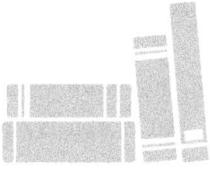

INTRODUCTION TO THE VIRGINIAN

INTRODUCTION

It is traditional that whenever a novel is published a few readers, reviewers or critics immediately associate the fictional characters with some real persons. So rampant is this custom that nearly every novelist carefully states that his characters have no resemblance to any person, living or dead and if such a similarity exists, it is purely accidental and totally unintentional. When it was published in 1902, *The Virginian* fell victim to the usual guessing game. Many readers thought the hero was based on Theodore Roosevelt; because the hero was favorably portrayed several elderly cowboys in the West claimed that Wister had based his character on their lives. It became necessary for Wister to clarify the matter in an introductory note addressed to the reader. Of course, like many fictional heroes, Wister's *Virginian* was a composite picture of several real people and the author's imagination.

"HISTORICAL NOVEL"

The first problem which Wister clarified for the reader was that of the time period which the novel covers. After an allusion to the original subtitle of the novel and a jibe at the culture of the East, Wister admits that his story is a historical one: "Any narrative which presents faithfully a day and a generation is of necessity historical; and this one presents Wyoming between 1874 and 1890." The original subtitle of the novel was "*A Tale of Sundry Adventures*". As we have said before, several **episodes** and chapters originally appeared as short stories. While the original subtitle is a truer reflection of the structure of the novel, it was replaced with the subtitle which has come down to us: *"A Horseman of the Plains".* Certainly the later subtitle is more in keeping with Wister's purpose of directing the reader's attention to the novel's hero rather than to individual adventures which occur in the course of the narrative. The new subtitle also prevents the casual reader from thinking the story is set in Virginia; also, we have the great symbol of the West, "a horseman," set against the vast natural background of the story, "the plains" of Wyoming.

"A VANISHED WORLD"

Wister goes on, in his introduction, to tell us that the Wyoming territory of the 1870s and 1880s is gone forever. If we were to travel to Cheyenne, "you would stand at the heart of the world that is the subject of my picture, yet you would look around you in vain for the reality. It is a vanished world." If Wister's remarks were true in 1902, how much more so they are true today. Although the mountains, sunlight and "infinite earth" are still there, "the buffalo...the wild antelope...and the horseman with his pasturing thousands" can exist only in our memories and imaginations. Of the horseman, Wister laments: "He rides in his historic yesterday. You will no more see him gallop out of the unchanging silence than you will see Columbus on the unchanging sea come sailing from Palos with his caravels."

Wister's lament was perhaps not necessary, since today, the cowboy lives on in American myth, from the cowboy and Indian games of young children to the highly creative imitations in art, literature, and music, from the ever popular Western movie and television productions to the medium of advertising in which the Western background and the heroic stature of the cowboy is employed to sell cigarettes, cigars, automobiles, clothes, etc.

"HERO WITHOUT WINGS"

The remainder of Wister's introduction is devoted to a romantic interpretation of the horseman of the plains and to a denial that he is based on a single living person. Wister's description of "the last romantic figure upon our soil" as he calls the cowboy, once again shows us several characteristics of Wister's writing. Note Wister's fascination with the cowboy's language, his realistic interpretation of certain phases of frontier life and then his romantic interpretation of the cowboy's traits as part of the American character. The final sentence of the passage is as excellent a description of the **theme** and hero of the novel as we can find:

> **Whatever he did, he did with his might. The bread that he earned was earned hard, the wages that he squandered were squandered hard, - half a year's pay sometimes gone in a night, - "blown in," as he expressed it, or "blowed in," to be perfectly accurate. Well, he will be here among us always, invisible, waiting his chance to live and play as he would like. His wild kind has been among us always, since the beginning: a young man with his temptations, a hero without wings.**

REDEDICATION

Ten years after the novel was published, Wister added a "Rededication and Preface" to the latest edition. The contents of this rededication reflect Wister's changing interests; he is no longer concerned with *The Virginian* and the **epic** cowpuncher or the heroic horseman of the plains, rather he uses this opportunity to express his political opinions. He compares Theodore Roosevelt to Abraham Lincoln and celebrates both as the great benefactors of America. Wister now considers *The Virginian* "an expression of American faith." Written in 1911, the rededication adds nothing to the novel and for our purposes-of analyzing the novel-it is vastly inferior to the original preface and dedication. However, it once again attests to the friendship between Wister and Roosevelt.

SETTING FOR THE VIRGINIAN

Wister chose Wyoming as the setting for *The Virginian* because it was the first part of the West with which he had become familiar. His first several trips there were before Wyoming had been granted statehood. The name Wyoming derives from an Indian word which means "the Plain". In one of the passages above Wister stated that immigrants came west "in shoals." The figurative term is accurate when we look at the census figures which cover the period of the story. In 1880, the first year for which we have census figures for Wyoming, the population was a mere 20,789. Ten years later, when the Wyoming Territory was admitted to statehood, the population had tripled and is recorded at 62,555. By 1960, the population was 330,066. The state has remained constant in size and includes 97,914 square miles making it the tenth largest of the fifty states in area. In the novel Wister constantly emphasizes the size of the territory. For example, Judge Henry's ranch is 263 miles from the railroad at Medicine Bow where the narrator meets the Virginian.

Cheyenne, the capital and largest city of the state, was settled in 1867 by engineers of the Union and Pacific railroad. As a rail center, Cheyenne quickly became a thriving "cow town" where herds of cattle and sheep entrained for Eastern markets. In his first preface, Wister locates the city at the center of the setting of his tale: "Had you left New York or San Francisco at ten o'clock this morning, by noon the day after tomorrow you could step out at Cheyenne. There you would stand at the heart of the world that is the subject of my picture..." It is important to remember that Wister's world is the general Wyoming territory and not the state as we know it. For as one can see on any map, Cheyenne is located in the south-eastern part of the state. Many other place names in the state reflect aspects of its history; for example, place names such as Emigrant Gap, Devil's Gate, Muddy Gap, Whiskey Gap, Horse Creek, Tie Siding, Cody, Laramie and Rawhide point up certain periods in Wyoming history.

MEDICINE BOW, WYOMING

This town is one of the places which Wister visited his first summer in the West. We learn from his journal entry for July 19, 1885 that he arrived there after a nineteen-hour ride. The description of the town in his journal is repeated practically verbatim in the novel:

> Town, as they called it, pleased me the less, the longer I saw it. But until our language stretches itself and takes in a new word of closer fit, town will have to do for the name of such a place as was Medicine Bow. I have seen and slept in many like it

since. Scattered wide, they littered the frontier from the Columbia to the Rio Grande, from the Missouri to the Sierras. They lay stark, dotted over a planet of treeless dust, like soiled packs of cards. Each was similar to the next, as one old five-spot of clubs resembles another. Houses, empty bottles, and garbage, they were forever of the same shapeless pattern. More forlorn they were than stale bones. They seemed to have been strewn there by the wind and to be waiting till the wind should come again and blow them away. Yet serene above their foulness swam a pure and quiet light such as the East never sees; they might be bathing in the air of creation's first morning. Beneath sun and stars their days and nights were immaculate and wonderful... Medicine Bow was my first, and I took its dimensions, twenty-nine buildings in all, one coal chute, one water tank, the station, one store, two eating-houses, one billiard hall, two tool-houses, one feed stable, and twelve others that for one reason and another I shall not name. Yet this wretched husk of squalor spent thought upon appearances; many houses in it wore a false front to seem as if they were two stories high. There they stood, rearing their pitiful masquerade amid a fringe of old tin cans, while at their very doors began a world of crystal light, a land without end, a space across which Noah and Adam might come straight from Genesis.

This passage is a mixture of factual reporting and the author's own opinion. While he factually reports that these frontier "towns" litter the West like soiled packs of cards and he chooses to emphasize their stark, dusty, shapeless patterns strewn with empty bottles and garbage, he nevertheless prefers them to the East because the cleanliness and freshness of the air and nature make them "immaculate and wonderful." The passage is a good example of Wister's romantic interpretation of a scene which he himself describes in terms such as "litter," "garbage" and "squalor." This dichotomy between reality and romance, the world as it is and the world as it ought to be exist throughout the novel. The town of Medicine Bow, like the character of the Virginian, is meant to be symbolic of a thousand other frontier towns of the time.

HISTORICAL AND ECONOMIC BACKGROUND

The Western territories were influenced by several important trends during the 1870s and 1880s. Some of these included the tremendous influx of Union and Confederate veterans who were unable to readjust to their native regions after the war. They sought the prizes and adventure which the great territory offered. By 1890, six states - North Dakota (November 2, 1889), South Dakota (November 2, 1889), Montana (November 8, 1889), Washington (November 11, 1889), Idaho (July 3, 1890), and Wyoming (July 10, 1890) - had been added to the Union, raising the number of states to thirty-four. Together with the Civil War veterans came thousands of immigrants, first to work on the railroads and later to become the backbone of agricultural America.

The era of great cattle drives followed the Chisholm or Western trails from the grasslands of Texas to the railroad centers at Abilene and Dodge City, Kansas, and Ogallala, Nebraska. A third major cattle trail, the Goodnight-Loving trail ended at Cheyenne, Wyoming. It has been estimated that between the close of the Civil War and 1890 more than 4,000,000 steers were driven to the rail centers and then to stockyards at Kansas City or Chicago.

This period was also the era of the last of the great buffalo herds and the great Indian Wars. The names of George A. Custer, Buffalo Bill Cody and Wild Bill Hickok are synonymous with the tempo of the times. In transportation the pace was just as rapid. The horse and prairie schooner dominated the early part of the period, but soon the wagon trains yielded to the transcontinental railroads for the longer distances. The first transcontinental railroad was completed in 1869; by 1893 there were five. At the end of the novel we learn that by 1892 the railroad had even reached Judge Henry's ranch. The conflict of cattle baron, sheep farmer and homesteader, the wily ways of land speculation, the emergence of railroad empires and Horace Greeley's 1850 maxim "Go west, young man, and grow with the country" were the prevailing movements of the day. Much of the land, opportunity and exuberance were gone in 1890, but this only encouraged the quicker rise of Western cities and institutions and the emergence of the great American farm and dairy lands. Of course, the period did not end exactly in 1890. Western states were admitted to the Union as late as 1912, when Arizona became the forty-eight state.

WISTER ON THE TRANSITION

In his 1902 preface, Wister commented on the change which had taken place:

> **A transition has followed the horseman of the plains; a shapeless state, a condition of men and manners unlovely as that bald moment in the year when winter is gone and spring not come, and the face of Nature is ugly. I shall not dwell upon it here. Those who have seen it know well what I mean. Such transition was inevitable. Let us give thanks that it is but a transition, and not a finality.**

Wister, as a student of history, realized that just as his horseman of the plains had vanished, so too, what followed him would vanish in its turn. History must sometimes be viewed as a cycle of equitable replacements, especially in the worlds of technology and industry. In our own time we have seen the automobile, truck and airplane displace the railroads as the principal method of travel and trade.

POINT OF VIEW IN THE VIRGINIAN

For the most part the story is told by the first person narrator. He is a visitor to the West and soon earns the epithet of "tenderfoot" because of his inexperience. However, before the story ends, the tenderfoot learns to hold his own with the most veteran cowpunchers. The author also enters the flow of the narrative at will; sometimes his purpose is to add a new dimension to the action, at other times Wister uses the technique to underscore a moral or to foreshadow a coming event. The technique of flashback is also employed by Wister. He will carry the story of one character or incident to a certain point and then turn to another character in order to bring the reader up to date on his activities.

CHAPTER DIVISION

Wister's use of chapter titles is an aid to the reader. Only five of the chapter titles stem directly from the dialogue of the story. These five reveal the plot in briefest terms: "When You Call Me That, Smile!" (Chapter 2), "You're Going to Love Me Before We Get Through" (Chapter 11), "Would You Be A Parson?" (Chapter 18), "What Is A Rustler?" (Chapter 22), and "To Fit Her Finger" (Chapter 34). The title of Chapter 2 has become the most famous line in the novel; it also reveals the conflict between the Virginian and Trampas. Two of the chapter titles (11 and 34) concern the Virginian's courtship of Molly Stark Wood. "Would You Be A Parson?" (Chapter 18) concerns one of the many humorous pranks perpetrated by the Virginian while "What Is A Rustler?" gives the author an opportunity to poke fun at static Eastern culture while revealing the sparkling speech in orations of frontier life.

Many chapter titles read like stage directions. For example, "Enter the Man" (Chapter 1) and "Enter the Woman" (Chapter 5) introduce the hero and heroine. In discussing Molly Stark Wood's Eastern heritage and the Virginian's chivalry Wister chooses the phrase: "Where Fancy Was Bred" (Chapter 10). Some titles are merely place names or geographical points of reference. Among these are "Deep Into Cattle Land" (Chapter 4), "Word to Bennington" (Chapter 29), "The Cottonwoods" (Chapter 31), and "Superstition Trail" (Chapter 32). Wister labels Chapters 13–16 as "acts": "The Game and the Nation - Act First" (Chapter 13), "Between the Acts" (Chapter 14), "The Game and the Nation - Act Second" (Chapter 15), and "The Game and the Nation - Last Act" (Chapter 16). Wister is not averse to making his chapter titles quite **didactic** as can be seen by such titles as "In a State of Sin" (Chapter 21) and "Progress of the Lost Dog". The "Lost Dog", as we shall see, refers to one of the characters. Three chapters dealing with Molly Stark Wood use the nineteenth century term for a single woman - spinster; "The Sincere Spinster" (Chapter 8), "The Spinster Meets The Unknown" (Chapter 9) and "The Spinster Loses Some Sleep" (Chapter 33). When Wister wishes to bring several characters or incidents up to date he merely entitles the chapter "Various Points" (Chapter 23). Occasionally the chapter bears the name of the main character of the incident as in "Em'ly" (Chapter 6) an egregious hen or "Balaam and Pedro" (Chapter 26), the story of a harsh master and an innocent horse.

ALLUSIONS IN THE VIRGINIAN

As can be seen from the last chapter title, Wister uses **allusions** quite freely throughout the novel. An author uses the literary device of **allusions** when he wishes to refer the reader to a person or thing which will add a new dimension to what he is saying. For example, in the title of Leon Uris' book *Exodus* we immediately recognize the Biblical **allusion** to the second book of the Old Testament in which Moses leads the people of Israel out of bondage in Egypt. With this knowledge the reader enjoys Exodus all the more as he draws parallels between the ancient journey to the promised land and the more modern one described by Uris. Wister uses Biblical, classical, historical and literary **allusions** in the novel. In Chapter 26, mentioned above, the reader will gain a quicker insight into the **episode** if he recognizes that "Balaam" is a Biblical **allusion** to an old heathen enchanter who beat the donkey he was riding (Numbers, xxii: 5 ff). Scipio Le Moyne is given the first name of the famous Roman general in order to add to Wister's caricature. The name of Judge Henry's prize stallion "Paladin" is also a historical allusion.

HISTORICAL AND LITERARY ALLUSIONS

The largest number of **allusions** in the novel are to people and incidents in American history and to titles, characters and lines in literary classics. The principal **allusions** to American history concern Molly Stark Wood and her New England background. Wister tells us that Molly, "had she so wished...could have belonged to any number of those patriotic societies of which our American ears have grown accustomed to hear so much. She could have been enrolled in the Boston Tea Party, the Ethan Allen Ticonderogas, the Green Mountain Daughters, the Saratoga

Sacred Aide, and the Confederated Chatelaines. She traced direct descent from the historic lady whose name she bore, that Molly Stark who was not a widow after the battle where her lord, her Captain John, battled so bravely as to send his name thrilling down through the blood of generations of schoolboys."

While Wister humorously treats the stereotyped patriotic organizations, membership in which is determined by birthright rather than merit or achievement, he is careful to inform us that Molly Wood declined membership in any of these organizations. The ancestor for whom Molly was named was the wife of General John Stark (1728–1822), the Revolutionary War hero. Uttering the words, "There are the Red Coats and they are ours, or this night Molly Stark sleeps a widow," General Stark led his men to victory against the forces of British General John Burgoyne on August 16, 1777 at the Battle of Bennington. To this day, August 16 is an official state holiday in Vermont. From these brave ancestors Molly inherited the pluck and pride which she exhibits in the course of the story whenever the situation demands extraordinary strength and courage on her part.

Historical **allusions** are also used to add autobiographical details to the Virginian's life. In his letter to Molly's mother he talks of his family: "We have fought when we got the chance, under Old Hickory and in Mexico and my father and two brothers were killed in the Valley sixty-four." "Old Hickory" refers to Andrew Jackson who won fame as an Indian fighter and as the defender of New Orleans in the War of 1812. "Mexico" refers to the Mexican War in 1846–1848 and "the Valley sixty-four", of course, refers to the part of the Civil War which was fought in 1864 in the Virginian's native state. Among them, Molly Wood's and the Virginian's ancestors had fought in every major war in the history of the country. Wister ends the novel with an

allusion to the Wyoming "cattle war of 1892", but the Virginian is shrewd enough to survive and grow with the times.

SOME LITERARY ALLUSIONS

When the Virginian begins to borrow books from Molly, the author is able to introduce many literary allusions. He alludes mostly to Shakespeare and popular nineteenth century English poets and novelists. Some of the more humorous sections of the novel occur when the Virginian begins to interpret a few literary classics to the narrator. His disregard for formal education, his concern for practical matters, and his tendency to analogy - turning everything he reads into the terms of his own western, democratic world - govern his criticisms and comments on literature. A selection from Chapter 13 will illustrate some of these points:

> *[The Virginian]* took out Sir Walter's Kenilworth once more, and turned the volume over and over slowly, without opening it. You cannot tell if in spirit he wandered on Bear Creek with the girl whose book it was. The spirit will go one road, and the thought another, and the body its own way sometimes. "Queen Elizabeth would have played a mighty pow'ful game," was his next remark."
>
> Poker?", said I.
>
> "Yes, seh. Do you expaict Europe has got any queen equal to her at present?"
>
> I doubted it.

"Victoria'd get pretty nigh slain sliding chips out agaynst Elizabeth. Only mos' probly Victoria she'd insist on a half-cent limit. You have read this hyeh Kenilworth? Well, deal Elizabeth ace high, an' she could scare Robert Dudley with a full house plumb out o' the bettin'." I said that I believed she unquestionably could.

"And," said the Virginian, "if Essex's play got next her too near, I reckon she'd have stacked the cyards. Say, d' yu' remember Shakespeare's fat man?"

"Falstaff? Oh, yes, indeed."

"Ain't that grand? Why, he makes men talk the way they do in life. I reckon he couldn't get printed to-day. It's a right down shame Shakespeare couldn't know about poker. He'd have had Falstaff playing all day at that Tearsheet outfit. And the Prince would have beat him."

"Something About Something": Wister's use of literary allusions reaches its high point as Molly reads some selections to the Virginian while he is recovering from his adventure with Balaam in the mountains. Molly reads him some selections from Jane Austen's novel, Emma, but the staid contents of the book quickly put the Virginian to sleep. Later he is critical of Browning's poetry because it is unrealistic although he does concede that "that writer does know something". During this talk the Virginian states his philosophy of literary value - a book must be "something about something." In other words, it must be realistic and have some practical relationship to one's own life. He uses Shakespeare's *Henry the Fourth* as an example of a literary work which means "something," and concludes: "that play is bed-rock, ma'am!"

Humor In *The Virginian*: Second only to its Western setting, humor is the mainstay of the novel. While some of the scenes tend to be dated, the broad outlines of most of the comical situations are easily comprehended. The Virginian is a teller of tales, a needler, and a practical joker. His humor and practical jokes are never meant to be harmful. He shows infinite patience and ingenuity in the conception and execution of his various schemes. Some of the better scenes are the exchanging of various babies' clothes at the dance, his "Em'ly" tale, his outwitting of Trampas and his duping of the parson. The Virginian's humor ranges from a pun and one line quip to the involved story and complex practical joke and finally to that deadly ambivalent type of comic seriousness as seen in the famous line, "When you call me that, smile!" or his mock pride when he informs Molly early in the story, "You're going to love me before we get through."

It is in these techniques of humor and literary **allusions** that Owen Wister's work most resembles the writings of Mark Twain. Twain also used a humorous interpretation of literary classics, a distrust of formal education and "civilization" in general, and a debunking of European aristocracy and Victorian staidness in *Huckleberry Finn*. We know that Wister was familiar with Twain's writings and that the elder writer had sent him a laudatory letter when the young Wister published his first novel. However, the differences between the two novelists are great since Twain came from the milieu about which he wrote while Wister wrote as a visitor to a strange, new land from the point of view of a cultured and Victorian gentleman. Twain was content to reveal a new regionalism in American literature; Wister, on the other hand, attempted to fit his new found West into the mainstream of Victorian literature.

Diction And Dialogue In *The Virginian*: Occasionally the reader will discover a phrase or word which is no longer used in the sense which Wister intended. However, the context usually makes the meaning clear. For example, today we seldom use the words "toilet" or "waistcoat" as Wister uses them in this description: "...before quitting the store, he made his toilet for this little hand at poker. It was a simple preparation. He took his pistol from its holster, examined it, then shoved it between his overalls and his shirt in front, and pulled his waistcoat over it. He might have been combing his hair for all the attention anyone paid to this..." Some other examples of the nineteenth century **diction** which has been replaced by modern equivalents include: "drummer" (salesman), "tins" (canned or packaged foods), and "biscuit-shooter" (cook).

Another interesting linguistic characteristic of the novel is the use of Western language. Today, the early West has been so assimilated into our experience that we have no difficulty knowing the meaning of a long list of Western words such as "badlands", "butte", "canon", "mustang", "corral", "cowpuncher", "bronco buster", "tinhorn" and "rustler". Many of these words are recorded by the Dictionary of American English as first entering the language during the 1800s. It took another several generations to make them part of the general vocabulary. As late as 1884, authors of histories and travel books felt it necessary to define these words for their readers.

In Chapter 22, "What Is A Rustler?" Wister relates a humorous incident at the expense of Molly's relatives who fear that Molly is engaged to a rustler. In reply to the question, "What is a rustler?" Wister tells us:

> **It was not in any dictionary, and current translations of it were inconsistent. A man at Hoosic Falls said that he had passed through Cheyenne, and heard the term applied in a complimentary way to people who**

were alive and pushing. Another man had always supposed it meant some kind of horse. But the most alarming version of all was that a rustler was a cattle thief.

Now the truth is that all these meanings were right. The word ran a sort of progress in the cattle country, gathering many meanings as it went. It gathered more, however, in Bennington. In a very few days, gossip had it that Molly was engaged to a gambler, a gold miner, an escaped stage robber, and a Mexican bandit; while Mrs. Flynt feared she had married a Mormon.

Wister's comment that the word "gathered many meanings in its history" is a linguistic fact. The meaning of the word as we know it today, namely "cattle thief" came into the language at the end of the nineteenth century according to the Dictionary of American English, whose earliest citation in this sense is dated 1893.

The principal dialect in the novel is that of the Virginian who, naturally, speaks in a Southern dialect. Wister creates this characteristic in two ways. The first is the commentary of the narrator who describes the hero's speech habits several times. Secondly, the dialogue of the Virginian is intended to simulate the Southern dialect. As a result, we find that the spelling of certain of the Virginian's words is the means of indicating the Southern speech dialect; for example, he uses "yu" for you, "cyard" for card, "gyarments" for garments, "seh" for sir, "hyeh" for here, etc.

One of the shortcomings of the novel is the dialogue. For, while Wister reflects dialects, the grammar and **syntax** are those of an educated man. The dialogue seems artificial and stilted and does not really catch the emotions of the speakers as we can see in this famous scene from Chapter 11:

> Molly Wood was regarding him saucily. "I don't think I like you," said she.
>
> "That's all square enough. You're goin' to love me before we get through. I wish yu'd come a-ridin' ma'am."
>
> "Dear, dear, dear! So I'm going to love you? How will you do it? I know men think that they only need to sit and look strong and make chests at a girl-"
>
> "Goodness gracious! I ain't makin' any chests at yu'!" Laughter overcame him for a moment, and Miss Wood liked his laugh very much. "Please come a-ridin'," he urged. "It's the prettiest kind of a day."
>
> She looked back at him frankly, and there was a pause. "I will take back two things that I said to you," she then answered him. "I believe that I do like you. And I know that if I went riding with you, I should not have an immature protector." And then, with a final gesture of acknowledgment, she held out her hand to him. "And I have always wanted," she said, "to thank you for what you did at the river."
>
> He took her hand, and his heart bounded. "You're a gentleman!" she exclaimed.

However, Wister can also achieve dramatic intensity through dialogue as is seen in an early scene in the story when the

Virginian calls Trampas for the first time. When Trampas curses the Virginian during a card game, the Virginian draws his pistol, holding it unaimed: "...With a voice as gentle as ever, the voice that sounded almost like a caress, but drawling a very little more than usual, so that there was a space between each word, he issued his orders to the man Trampas: -'When you call me that, smile'!" The tension of the scene is allowed to build for a moment as the room fills with deadening silence. Then almost as quickly, Trampas, by his inaction, chooses not to "draw his steel" against the Virginian. A transition is made between this scene and later ones as the narrator comments: "A public back down is an unfinished thing..." As we see, the scene is not really finished until the final showdown at the end of the story when the Virginian says after his gunfight with Trampas, "I expect that's all."

EPIGRAMMATIC STYLE

Another characteristic of Wister's style is that of weaving epigrammatic statements into the fabric of the narrative. Epigrams are pointed sayings, akin to adages, which state a truth or perhaps a paradox. Wister uses these sayings freely in the novel. A few examples would include:

> "We cannot see ourselves as others see us." (Chapter 2)
>
> "It's not a brave man that's dangerous...it's the cowards that scare me." (Chapter 3)
>
> "A valise is a poor companion for catching a train with." (Chapter 14)

"If words were meant to conceal our thoughts, melody is perhaps a still thicker veil for them." (Chapter 18)

"And it may be safely surmised that if a bird of any particular feather has been for a long while unable to see other birds of its kind, it will flock with them all the more assiduously when they happen to alight in its vicinity." (Chapter 22)

"But all men grasp at straws." (Chapter 23)

"In bets, in card games, in all horse transactions and other matters of similar business, a man must take care of himself, and wiser onlookers must suppress their wisdom and hold their peace." (Chapter 25)

"...all accepted lovers have to face this ordeal of being treated like specimens by the other family." (Chapter 29)

"...many things in this world should be done in silence..."

(Chapter 33)

"...no earthly foot can step between a man and his destiny." (Chapter 35)

A LIST OF CHARACTERS

Although the major characters are discussed in detail in a later section of the outline, this list of most of the characters who appear in the novel will aid the reader in following the plot analysis.

The Stranger

Nicknamed "the Prince of Wales" because of his English clothes and "the tenderfoot" because of his inexperience, this cultivated Easterner narrates much of the story.

The Virginian

The hero of the story; his fortunes are the main concern of the novel.

Uncle Hughey

A prospective bridegroom at Medicine Bow.

Steve

A friend of the Virginian's, proprietor of the general store at Medicine Bow; later he is hanged for rustling.

TWO JEWISH "DRUMMERS"

A Traveling Cigar Salesman

He's spending the night in Medicine Bow.

Dutch-German "Drummer"

Traveling "jew'lry" salesman.

American "Drummer"

Traveling patent medicine salesman whose product is named "Consumption Killer". He is the butt of the Virginian's practical joke.

A Railroad Employee

Occupant of the fifth bed at the Medicine Bow "hotel".

Union Pacific Agent

Stationmaster at Medicine Bow.

Mrs. Glen

Proprietor of the eating-house and "hotel" at Medicine Bow and an admirer of the Virginian.

Trampas

An unsavory "tin-horn" who insults the Virginian during a poker game. The stock villain of the story, he provokes the Virginian at various times until the two inevitably face one another in a gun duel at the end of the novel.

A Card Dealer

The moralizing sage at the saloon in Medicine Bow.

The Engineer's Wife

A sick woman at Medicine Bow for whom the cowboys show consideration.

Buck And Mullins

Judge Henry's team of horses.

Balaam

A maltreater of horses.

Mrs. Balaam

His wife and the initial correspondent with Molly Wood.

Charlie Taylor

A leading citizen of Bear Creek.

Mrs. Taylor

His wife, an admirer of the Virginian and advisor to Molly.

Judge Henry

The narrator's friend and owner of the Sunk Creek Ranch.

Mrs. Henry

His wife; he affectionately calls her Mrs. Judge.

Em'ly

An egregious fowl at the ranch.

Paladin

The Judge's imported stallion.

Honey Wiggin, Nebrasky, Dollar Bill, Chalkeye

Cow punchers at the Sunk Creek Ranch.

Molly Stark Wood

The heroine of the story, who leaves her native Bennington, Vermont, to teach in Bear Creek, Wyoming.

Mrs. John Stark

Molly's mother.

Sam Bannett

Molly's suitor from Hoosic, New York.

Mrs. Flynt

Wife of the Baptist minister in Bennington, Vermont.

The Episcopal Rector

Molly's friend in Hoosic, New York.

Molly's Great-Aunt

Her affectionate advisor from Dunbarton, New Hampshire.

Alfred And Christopher

Mr. and Mrs. Westfall's children.

Monte

The Virginian's horse.

Mr. And Mrs. Westfall, Mr. And Mrs. Taylor, Mr. And Mrs. Thomas, Mr. And Mrs. Carmody, Mr. And Mrs. Dow, The Swinton Brothers

Families of Bear Creek, Wyoming

Andrew Bell

Molly's brother-in-law.

Sarah Bell

His wife, Molly's sister.

Lin Mclean

A friend of the Virginian's and a suitor of Molly's.

Bokay Baldy

Another suitor of Molly's.

Old Judge Barrage

Another of Molly's suitors.

Bob Carmody, Henry Dow, George Taylor

Molly's students at the Bear Creek Schoolhouse.

Shorty

A kind of drifter, misled by Trampas.

Pedro

Shorty's horse, his prized possession which he later sells to Balaam.

Dr. Alexander Macbride

A traveling missionary who comes to the Judge's ranch.

Mr. And Mrs. Ogden

Visitors from New York who visit with the Judge at Sunk Creek Ranch.

Scipio Le Moyne

A colorful drifter whom the Virginian makes his cook.

Ed

Steve's fellow rustler; he is also hanged.

The Bishop

Officiates at the marriage of the Virginian and Molly.

Scenes In *The Virginian*

There are two principal groups of scenes in the novel; first, those which take place in the Bennington, Vermont, area and concern the background and family of Molly Stark Wood and second, those which take place against the gigantic background of the Wyoming territory and surrounding states at the time of the story. Wister occasionally uses multiple scenes within one chapter but this is not a usual procedure for him. Also, he will include a chapter in which the scene can only be described as "in the East" or "in the West". The following outline itemizes the settings of the scenes chapter by chapter; this has been determined by using the place where most of the action in the chapter occurs. Wister brings the diverse settings and scenes together in the last chapter of the book.

Chapters Scene-Setting

1–3   Medicine Bow, Wyoming

4–5   The 263 mile journey from Medicine Bow to the Judge's ranch

6   The Sunk Creek Ranch

7	An anonymous Eastern city
8	Bennington, Vermont Dunbarton, New Hampshire Hoosic, New York
9	The range near Sunk Creek; Molly's journey from Bennington, Vermont to Bear Creek
10	A Saturday night dance and barbecue at the Swinton Brothers' Goose Egg outfit; Sunday at Molly's cabin in Bear Creek
11–12	Bennington, Vermont Bear Creek, Wyoming
13	Omaha, Nebraska
14–16	The Virginian's return trip from Chicago to the ranch
18–21	Sunk Creek Ranch
22	Bennington, Vermont; Sunk Creek, Wyoming
23–24	Sunk Creek and Bear Creek, Wyoming
25	Balaam's Ranch
26	Journey from Balaam's Ranch to Sunk Creek
27–29	The mountains and Molly's cabin; Bennington, Vermont
30–32	Idaho and Wyoming territory

33-35 Sunk Creek and Bear Creek, Wyoming

36 The honeymoon in the mountains of Wyoming, a visit to Bennington and the return to Wyoming

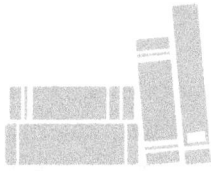

INTRODUCTION TO THE VIRGINIAN

TEXTUAL ANALYSIS

CHAPTERS 1-6

As the train from the East stops to take on water at Medicine Bow, Wyoming, the narrator of the story, as well as the other passengers, observes some activity in a trackside corral. Several cow ponies, and one maverick in particular, are "plunging, huddling, and dodging" about in an effort to escape the inevitable confinement of a wrangler's rope. As the cowboys take turns trying to rope the highly spirited horse, the scene offers great amusement to their fellows seated around the corral, as well as to the spectators on the train. The narrator notices one cowboy in particular; he is quiet and confident in contrast to the others. As he takes his turn with the rope, his manner, skill, control and reflexes easily make him successful in subduing the difficult horse. "That man knows his business," one of the passengers remarks as the train moves slowly to the station platform.

The narrator has little time to reflect on the scene or to comment since Medicine Bow is his destination. He has come from the East to visit Judge Henry, a friend, who owns a cattle ranch. He is to meet one of the Judge's men at the station. However, his mind is soon occupied with other problems, for just as the train is going out of sight, the stranger realizes that he has forgotten his trunk. His complaints to the baggage man are of no avail; the latter tells the stranger that the occurrence is not unusual since "passengers often got astray from their trunks, but the trunks mostly found them after a while." The narrator's annoyance is interrupted as he listens to a humorous conversation between the quiet cowboy from the corral and Uncle Hughey, a perennial bridegroom who always seems to be left at the altar. The cowboy has the appearance of having traveled a long way in the dusty country, but the narrator observes that "no dinginess of travel or shabbiness of attire could tarnish the splendor that radiated from his youth and strength." The cowboy's voice is "Southern and gentle and drawling."

After Uncle Hughey departs on the east-bound train to continue his persistent search for a bride, the cowboy approaches the stranger. He presents the guest with a letter of introduction from the Judge. The letter informs the stranger that the cowboy, whom we shall hereafter know only as the Virginian, is a trustworthy man and will bring him safely to the Sunk Creek Ranch. The stranger is impressed with the physical appearance of the Virginian but does not know how to cope with his quick wit, as can be seen by this brief exchange:

He answered slowly, "Then you have it correct, seh."

A slight chill passed over my easiness, but I went cheerily on with a further inquiry. "Find many oddities out here like Uncle Hughey?"

"Yes, seh, there is a right smart of oddities around. They come in on every train."

At this point I dropped my method of easiness.

Because the journey to the ranch is two hundred and sixty-three miles, the Virginian suggests that they spend the night in town. (For a description of Medicine Bow, see the selection on page 20).

Comment

In this section we are introduced to the **protagonist** and to the narrator of the tale. The latter is amorphous and shadowy; we never learn very much about him except that he is young and has the wherewithal to travel about the country almost as he pleases. The Virginian, on the other hand, is richly described, both in appearance and in personality. Being not a real man, but the personification of the Old West as seen through the starry eyes of an idealistic Easterner, the Virginian is more to be admired than believed in. Quite possibly the reason for his namelessness, his only appellations throughout the book being "the Virginian," "the Southerner" and the like, can be adduced from the fact that even Wister could not pretend that such a person existed or could exist; in a better (and more Westernized) America he would exist.

Upon comparing the people and places in *The Virginian* with those found in the works of Mark Twain, it is apparent that one's point of view is all-important. Twain, when describing the milieus from which he came or in which he worked, used a photographic eye and a phonographic ear. Even Huck Finn, who embodied the virtues and failings of many of Twain's boyhood friends, was real. One could almost reach out and touch him. Interestingly enough, this clarity of vision deserted Twain when he ranged further afield. The Mysterious Stranger is a fine work but it contains no character as human or palpable as Aunt Polly.

Wister, then, had the disadvantage of seeing Wyoming from the outside, as it were. It was new and breathlessly exciting to him, and even when, perhaps in an attempt to simulate verisimilitude, he ascribes faults to his "good" people, for example, the Virginian's puckish nature, these faults emerge as endearing traits.

On the way to the combination eating-house and "hotel" the Virginian meets Steve, an old friend and currently proprietor of the general store in Medicine Bow. Steve calls his friend "you old son-of-a _____" and tells him the five beds in the shack attached to the eating-house which serves as the hotel are all occupied for the night. The occupants are mostly "drummers", traveling salesmen. When Steve agrees to let the stranger sleep on the counter at his store, the Virginian bets Steve "a round of drinks" that he can dupe one of the drummers out of his bed. The rest of the evening with the exception of the Trampas incident is concerned with the machinations of the Virginian to secure a bed.

The Virginian chooses as his victim the American "drummer" whose product is called "Consumption Killer". After hoodwinking the salesman by feigning interest in patent medicines, the Virginian is offered a share of the drummer's bed. The cowboy accepts and says he will probably turn in after playing some cards. During the card game, an unsavory character named Trampas addresses the Virginian with the same phrase which Steve had used. But where Steve's use of the phrase was affectionate, Trampas' words were an intended insult. Drawing his gun, the Virginian replies to Trampas' "Your bet, you son of a _____" with his famous line, "When you call me that, smile!" Trampas does not challenge the Virginian, at least not this time. The stranger draws two conclusions about the events of his first night in the West. One concerns the Trampas incident, "A public backdown is an unfinished thing, - for some natures at least, I looked at his face, and thought it sullen, but tricky rather than courageous," and the other takes the form of an epigram. He has heard the Virginian called the same phrase by two different men. The Virginian laughed with Steve about it, but he drew on Trampas; the stranger concludes "that the letter means nothing until the spirit gives it life." In other words, the situation and purpose determine the appropriateness of any non-standard language.

When the Virginian gets into bed with the salesman he begins the second part of his plan to win his bet with Steve. Meanwhile, Steve, the stranger and several spectators are quietly awaiting the results of the hoax. He tells the drummer not to touch him because he suffers from nightmares; if anything disturbs him he'll probably react with knife and gun. The frightened salesman loses no time in abandoning the bed and as he trips on his own box of "Consumption Killer," the Virginian howls, the door bursts open and the sleepers are awakened and jostled about. It is clearly a case of the country boys outwitting "the city slickers" and the cowboys want to make an all night celebration of it. But news of a sick woman makes them chivalrously desist from their revelry. When Steve urges his old friend to drink some more, the Virginian declines saying, "I have got to stay responsible." As he retires that first evening in the West, the narrator wonders, "What world am I in?" and "Does this same planet hold Fifth Avenue?"

Before departing for the ranch the next morning the stranger noticed that Mrs. Glen, the owner of the eating-house and hotel, has a deep affection for the Virginian and later he notices a long blond hair on the Virginian's flannel shirt. Mrs. Glen, whose husband is away on the railroad, is a blond. Uncle Hughey arrives from Laramie, with his new bride and the town gives him a roaring welcome.

The two hundred and sixty-three mile trip takes four days. The long journey gives Wister an opportunity to interrupt the flow of the narrative with editorial comment such as:

The cow-boy is now gone to worlds invisible: the wind has blown away the white ashes of his camp-fires; but the empty sardine box lies rusting over the face of the Western earth.

He also interrupts after the stranger and the Virginian learn from Mr. Taylor that a new schoolmarm named Molly Stark Wood is coming from Bennington, Vermont, to teach school at Bear Creek. His purpose is to foreshadow the love affair between Molly and the Virginian; he discusses how the seeds of love are sown and how they bide their time before blooming.

Although the Virginian does not warm up to the stranger, the latter does, nevertheless, learn more about him as they travel together on this four-day ride. Besides the natural grandeur, abundant wildlife and magnificent air, the stranger experiences a day "in which we never passed a human being," a frightening ride behind the Judge's team as Buck panics when he smells and sees a branding fire, and the speed at which rumors and gossip travel, even in this country, seemingly without rapid communication. The Virginian tells the guest that Buck was once owned by Balaam, a maltreater of horses. The travelers hear the gossip when they meet Charlie Taylor from Bear Creek. It seems the Virginian pulled a gun in a poker game in order to win; at least that's the way Mr. Taylor heard it, but the source was probably Trampas even though Taylor heard it from a third party. Disclaiming any interest in the new schoolteacher and claiming even less interest in marriage, the Virginian nevertheless envisions Miss Wood as a woman about twenty years old and one who is insincere in her spinsterhood. Upon his arrival the stranger is warmly greeted by the Henrys. He sees little of the Virginian, although he would like to get to know him better. However, it is not long before a hen by the name of Em'ly draws the two men together.

Judge Henry's ranch at Sunk Creek is described as "an oasis in the Territory's desolate bill-of-fare." It abounds in trees and flowers because of a good water supply. The Judge has such a large number of cattle that they are described as "regiments" while his horses, sired by Paladin, his imported stallion, prosper and play in an eight-mile-square field of the richest grass. Soon the stranger's inexperience earns him the nickname-"tenderfoot". In turn the cowboys impress him as being composite characters diverse only in their names:

But the romance of America had drawn them all alike to this great playground of young men, and in their courage, their generosity, and their amusement at me they bore a close resemblance to each other.

The Virginian is assigned the task of caring for the tenderfoot. One day in the course of that duty, the Virginian relates some of the characteristics of Em'ly, one of the strangest hens he has ever seen. Em'ly is in the habit of sitting on potatoes, onions, soap or similar objects in an effort to hatch a chick; also she has an aversion to roosters. Soon she takes to expropriating another fowl's chicks and even tries the offspring of a different species when she seizes two baby turkeys. Finally she raises a litter of puppies for a lazy old setter, but when they are large enough they merely knock her down and abandon her. It becomes daily routine for the stranger and the Virginian to follow Em'ly's activities. Finally the Virginian borrows a nearly hatched egg and has Em'ly sit on it; within ten hours she has her own chick. Rather than being happy Em'ly ignores the chick and she dies shortly after. When the stranger departs for the East a few weeks later the Virginian's last words to him are that the story of Em'ly "is just one o' them parables." The parable in the novel is that Em'ly's plight aroused a common sympathy in these two men and made them life-long friends.

Comment

The expression, "When you call me that, smile," must surely be the best known and most enduring in Western literature (the origins of "They went thataway" and "We'll head 'em off at the pass" being obscured in the mists of time). Because, in at least one movie version, two Trampas-Virginian confrontations were telescoped into one, the line was changed to, "When you say that, smile," but it has lost none of its pungency.

Trampas is, of course, the villain of the piece, personifying what little venality Wister found in the West. His skulduggery, here and throughout the novel, seems as purposeless as Iago's, and his schemes are far less successful than those of the Moor's ancient.

Steve is not a well-drawn character. We are told that he is the Virginian's closest friend, but we must take this on faith. We cannot, ourselves, see or feel this friendship. This is a pity, for Steve, if more carefully portrayed, might have emerged as the most interesting person in the book.

The **episode** detailing the deception of the drummer contains ethnic references which might, perhaps, seem distasteful to the modern reader. It is well, however, to consider the time when they were written and the lack of importance Wister seems to attach to them. Doubtless, the entire scene seemed cleverer and more humorous than it does today.

Uncle Hughey, the precursor of Gabby Hayes, is introduced for comic relief and then, except for one or two brief reappearances, is quietly shunted aside for the rest of the novel. And a good thing, too.

The affair the Virginian has with Mrs. Glen, about which we learn obliquely, serves to remind us that he is not only a man's man but one who is attractive to women.

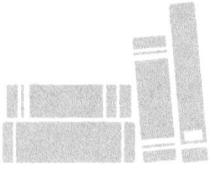

INTRODUCTION TO THE VIRGINIAN

TEXTUAL ANALYSIS

CHAPTER 7-12

Chapter 7, "Through Two Snows" is a transitional chapter in which we are given a summary of the past events, all of the characters are brought up to date and we are launched into the next major part of the story, in this case, the background and arrival in the West of the New England school-teacher-Molly Stark Wood. We learn that the stranger is in the East and that he has received a letter from the Virginian. Some strange change has occurred in the relationship of Steve and the Virginian since Steve is notable by his absence from mention in the Virginian's letter; also, Uncle Hughey is now the proud father of twins. Finally, the letter mentions that the Virginian has given up his job at the Sunk Creek Ranch but plans to return later when the Judge realizes his value. He chooses this plan of action rather than "stoop to telling tales out of school" which would be the case if he reported the men whose work he was doing.

That winter the Judge and his wife visit the East and the stranger learns that the Virginian is back at Sunk Creek, the schoolhouse at Bear Creek is nearly completed, the new teacher will arrive that spring, and that the Virginian and Steve parted company. While neither man will discuss the reason behind their strained relationship, it is rumored that Steve is involved, in some way, in cattle rustling.

Molly Stark Wood of Bennington, Vermont, has agreed to teach school in Bear Creek. Her mother and friends, especially Sam Bannett of Hoosic, New York, who wants to marry her, are upset that this proper New England girl plans to teach in "the wild west." But Molly is an unusual girl; she refuses to use her heritage (she is a direct descendant of the Revolutionary War patriot whose name she bears) for social advantage. Also, she is determined to make a mark on the world in her own way. From the age of twenty she has supported herself by embroidering handkerchiefs, making preserves and teaching music. Although the Woods had never been wealthy, they had been comfortable until the mills around Bennington experienced economic hardships. Because of her own independence, pluck and pride, Molly decided to accept the position in Wyoming. She packs a few personal belongings including her prized heirloom-a miniature portrait of the original Molly Stark painted when that Revolutionary lady was about twenty years old. Molly often looks at the portrait to see if the resemblance, which her great-aunt in Dunbarton, New Hampshire, is always noting, is really there.

At the same time that Molly is preparing to leave Bennington, we are given a description of the Virginian riding the range in the cold spring. His seriousness and reticence is occasionally interrupted when he sings a cowboy song which has seventy-nine verses, "seventy-eight of which were quite unprintable..." One day he visits his old friend, Jim Westfall; the Westfalls, who have been married about three years, have two children, Alfred and Christopher. Mrs. Westfall feeds the cowpunchers and tells them it is time "for all of them to become husbands like James." But the Virginian is not about to heed her advice as we learn from this passage:

> **The bachelors of the saddle listened, always diffident, but eating heartily to the end; and soon after they rode away in a thoughtful clump. The wives of Bear Creek were few as yet, and the homes scattered; the schoolhouse was only a sprig on the vast face of a world of elk and bear and uncertain Indians; but that night, when the earth near the fire was littered with cowpunchers' beds, the Virginian was heard drawling to himself: "Alfred and Christopher. Oh sugar!" ...They found pleasure in the delicately chosen shade of this oath.**

Molly leaves Bennington at noon on a Monday. At Hoosic Junction she realizes that Sam Bannett is aboard the train. An enthusiastic suitor, Sam begs Molly to allow him to accompany her as far as Rotterdam Junction. But Molly refuses and Sam obeys her. The author chides Sam's indecision:

> **I should like to be sorry for him, but obedience was not a lover's part here. He hesitated, the golden moment hung hovering, the conductor cried "All aboard!" the train went, and there on the platform stood obedient Sam, with his golden moment gone like a butterfly.**

The author's remarks are a good contrast to what will be the Virginian's reaction in a similar situation. Molly's "through car" crosses New York State on Monday, Ohio on Tuesday, and by Thursday she is eating breakfast at North Platte, Nebraska. Late the fourth night she leaves the railroad at Rock Creek. The final leg of her journey begins by stagecoach at six in the morning.

Near the Bow Leg Mountains, the negligence of the stage driver, who has been drinking, causes the vehicle to sink in the mud of the river at South Fork. As the driver lashes the horses in vain, and the stage is slowly sinking deeper into the middle of the river, a tall rider (the Virginian) appears from nowhere, and snatching the startled spinster he carries her to the safety of the shore. The rider after saying something about "cheering up," and it's being "all right" then "gently withdrew." But before returning to the nearby herd, the mysterious rider relieves the stage driver of his bottle of whiskey and chastises him for his stupidity. When the Sunk Creek cowpunchers have pulled the stage to dry land, the driver has become a new man. He helps Molly into the stage and they continue on to Bear Creek. As Molly attempts to collect her thoughts about the four days of train travel, thirty hours of stage travel and the recent excitement at the river, she notices that she has lost her handkerchief, one embroidered with flowers. She recalls seeing the stranger who helped her put something in his pocket, but she dismisses the thought as a figment of her imagination. But, as we learn later, the Virginian had indeed taken Molly's handkerchief as a memento. He recreates the scene in his mind many times during the next few months, especially whenever he happens by the scene of the incident or looks at the handkerchief. Meanwhile Molly occupies a cabin which has been built for her next to the Taylors' house.

| Comment

Here we have one of many examples of Wister's unabashed use of coincidence. Having previously learned of her existence through her letter to Mrs. Balaam, the Virginian meets Molly Wood in the midst of the vast Western plains, providentially just in time to save her life. The incident is stranger still in that neither the rescued girl, nor her savior, deem it worth mentioning to a soul. Surely the saving of a human life was not so common an occurrence as that.

The Virginian does not see Molly until a dance and barbecue given by the Swinton brothers at the Goose Egg ranch. Molly has been plagued by suitors since she arrived in the territory but she has discouraged them all. Without her knowledge, the Virginian once again becomes her champion when he forces Trampas to apologize for some ungentlemanly remarks he makes about the new schoolmarm. The Virginian shows his chivalrous nature as he addresses Trampas and his fellow cowpunchers: "We ain't a Christian outfit a little bit, and maybe we have most forgotten what decency feels like. But I reckon we haven't plumb forgot what it means."

While the Virginian is Molly's champion in private, he is quite awkward and upset in their first "formal" meeting. When she first sees him at the dance she immediately thinks of the incident at South Fork and the missing handkerchief. Molly first chooses to ignore him and later refuses to dance with him because they have not been formally introduced. Being a man of action, the Virginian quickly has Mr. Taylor perform the proper introductions, but much to the hero's chagrin Molly turns her attentions to the other guests. Lin McLean, who has also been a victim of Molly's fickleness, shares his sadness with his friend, the Virginian. Soon the two friends have had too much to drink and plan a practical joke. The babies of all the guests are sleeping quietly in the storeroom behind the kitchen. In all there are ten or twelve babies and the two cowboys decide to exchange the babies' clothes so that the parents will mistakenly take the wrong children home. The joke works to perfection. When the party ends the parents depart, each with someone else's child. Most of them do not discover the hoax until they have driven the many miles to their homes. Once the discovery is made the parents hastily return to secure their own children and take vengeance upon the "kidnappers." It is not until ten o'clock the next morning that everyone is back at the Swinton ranch and clothes, babies and parents have been rightfully matched again. Because the day is beautiful and there is food left from the night before, the ire and vengeance of the parents slowly give way to mirth as the Virginian disarms the raging mothers by his full confession and a new party begins.

Later in the day the Virginian visits Molly. Their fierce independence and deep pride, as well as the cultural differences between these two characters, place many barriers between them. When Molly tells the Virginian, "I don't think I like you," the arrogant conceit of his reply "You're goin' to love me before we get through..." startles her so much that she begins to have second thoughts about her opinion of this tall, manly Southerner. She is even able to finally thank him for his help at their first meeting six months before. While she does not go riding with him on this Sunday afternoon, Molly does accept his invitation for a ride in the future. That night the dreams and thoughts of both characters are dominated by memories of each other; Molly wonders, "What color were his eyes?" and the Virginian muses, "I ain't too old for education. Maybe she will lend me books..."

Molly's letters to Bennington are quite detailed. In one she relates the incident about the switching of the babies. Her brother-in-law, Andrew Bell, wonders why she does not say who played the trick. In other letters she asks for books and tells about her improving skill at riding a spirited horse. Most of the Easterners feel sorry for Molly because she is living in a place they feel is "vulgar," "horrible" and "dreadful." Mrs. Wood's return letters urge Molly to be careful about her associates and be sure they are approved by Mrs. Balaam. Mrs. Wood could not grasp the reality that Mrs. Balaam lived a long day's journey away and Molly saw her only about once every three months. The books which Molly had requested, "Shakespeare, Tennyson, Browning, Longfellow; and a number of novels by Scott, Thackeray, George Eliot, Hawthorne, and lesser writers; some volumes of Emerson; and Jane Austen complete…," arrived at Bear Creek about a week before Christmas. By New Year's the Virginian had begun his "education." On their many rides together during the next few months Molly's discussions of literary works are tempered by the Virginian's wide experience and practical knowledge. For, while he is only four years older than she is chronologically, and they are equal in terms of personal resourcefulness, honor and courage, the Virginian is many years her senior when it comes to experience.

This is clearly shown in Chapter 12, "Quality and Equality," in which the concrete experience of the Virginian is clearly contrasted with the idealistic theories of Molly concerning the problems of equality and the future course of their own relationship. Molly supports the proposition that "All men are born equal." The Virginian points out that this is inconsistent with what she has already told him about her three students who have varying abilities. The cowboy has a rule of thumb to solve the problem of equality: "equality is a great big bluff. It's easy called…but a man has got to prove himself my equal before I'll believe him." Although Molly discourages his talk of love she does not want him to stop seeing her. The Virginian respects her honesty and says that when he comes again he will also be honest and will certainly be more nearly equal to her after all this reading.

Comment

At times, Wister is most didactic. Some of the conversations in the novel more closely resemble the *Dialogues of Plato* than ordinary conversation. This might be borne equably if the philosophy thus expounded were profound or thought-provoking. Wister's tenets, however, are quite elementary, bordering on the banal.

CHAPTERS 13-17

The author begins this group of chapters with a discussion of equality. His style is expository rather than fictional; he uses the adventures of the Virginian as an example of his thesis. Wister tells us that "All America is divided into two classes-the quality and the equality." Equality will never be a substitute for quality and "both will be with us until our women bear nothing but Kings." Of course, that day will never come.

How did this division come about? Wister tells us:

It was through the Declaration of Independence that we Americans acknowledged the eternal inequality of man. For by it we abolished a cut-and-dried aristocracy. We had seen little men artificially held up in high places, and great men artificially held down in low places, and our own justice-loving hearts abhorred this violence to human nature. Therefore, we decreed that every man should thenceforth have equal liberty to find his own level. By this very decree we acknowledged and gave freedom to true aristocracy, saying, "Let the best man win, whoever he is." Let the best man win! That is America's word. That is true democracy. And true democracy and true aristocracy are one and the same thing. If anybody cannot see this, so much the worse for his eyesight.

The questions about equality discussed in Chapters 12 and 13 are answered in the above passage by the line which tells us that every man should "have equal liberty to find his own level." His maxim, "Let the best man win," is the hallmark of individualism and in the novel is the guiding philosophy of the Virginian even though his experience had taught him that the best man did not always win. "Best" in Wister's sense is closely allied to "moral" in personal matters, "chivalrous" in social matters and "democratic" in political matters. Is the Virginian the best man? Yes. For, as the narrator tells us in Chapter 17, "It was at Billings, on this day, that I made those reflections about equality. For the Virginian had been equal to the occasion; that is the only kind of equality which I recognize."

Comment

Here the author, to some extent, eschews the device of talking through his characters and addresses the reader directly. Wister did not have the knack, possessed by greater figures in literature, of instructing while seeming only to entertain. A lesson is often easier to learn when we don't realize we are learning it and it is apt to stay with us longer. As W. S. Gilbert said, "He who'd make his fellow creature wise / Should always gild the philosophic pill."

The "occasion" to which the Virginian has been equal occupies the action described between the author's thesis of equality and his conclusion. The narrator has returned from the East. He unexpectedly meets the Virginian at Colonel Cyrus Jones' eating place in Omaha, Nebraska. The cowboy has changed in the past two years. His responsibilities as acting foreman involved delivering a herd of the Judge's cattle to Chicago. He was in charge of two ten-car trains and their double crew of cowboys. On the return trip the Virginian was to see certain officials of the Great Northern Railroad at St. Paul in an attempt to secure cheaper shipping rates for the Sunk Creek cattle. But the difficult responsibility was to get all the cowpunchers safely back to the ranch where the Judge needed their services for a second roundup. He had to keep the men away from the temptation of the cities through which they would pass on the return trip. The narrator comments on the physical changes he sees in his friend:

> **The boy was altogether gone from his face-the boy whose freak with Steve had turned Medicine Bow upside down, whose other freak with the babies had outraged Bear Creek, the boy who had loved to jingle his spurs. But manhood had only trained, not broken, his youth. It was all there, only obedient to the rein and curb.**

Another change which the narrator notices in his friend is his fascination with books. They discuss how Queen Elizabeth and Falstaff would play poker. The narrator finds it hard to tell whether the cowboy was concentrating on the contents of the book he is reading or whether he was daydreaming about the girl at Bear Creek whose book it was. The two separate once again; the Virginian continuing to Chicago, the Easterner traveling by rail to Fort Meade.

Comment

Although Wister's West is as big as all outdoors, it can conveniently diminish when he has occasion for two of his characters to meet. The entirely unforeseen encounter between the Virginian and the narrator at Col. Cyrus Jones's eating palace at Omaha, Nebraska, elicits not so much as, "Well, it's a small world," from either of them.

This is an example of the propensity of Wister's characters to speak and act not out of any compelling need from within themselves, but merely to further the plot. Quite possibly, this arose from the novel's genesis in previously written short pieces which Wister did not quite know how to bind together. The end result is not a great picaresque novel, in the tradition of Gil Blas or *Huckleberry Finn*, but a loosely strung together selection of essays, stories, and anecdotes of varying interest.

This is not to say that *The Virginian* is of no value. No work which depicts a bygone era or culture by an eye-witness should be spared our attention, however cursory. For all of Horatio Alger, Jr.'s mawkish sentimentality and cardboard characters, such books as Ragged Dick and Phil the Fiddler are worth reading, if only to learn a bit about certain aspects of life in New York in Alger's day.

Several days later, as the narrator and two traveling companions, Scipio le Moyne and Shorty, miss a train connection at Medora, we once again meet the Virginian. He is sitting on the rear platform of a caboose of a long freight train headed West. His steers were delivered and his crew was safely inside as the narrator could tell from the noise. The three travelers join the Virginian and the Sunk Creek outfit for the caboose trip further West.

As the train slowly begins on its journey, one of the Sunk Creek crew comes out of the caboose and begins an argument with the Virginian. The cowpuncher had wanted to get off at this stop to get a bottle of whiskey. Not a man to waste words, the Virginian kicks him off the train into the dust of Dakota. With his typical humor, the Virginian reflects "That is the only step I have had to take this whole trip." The man whom the deputy foreman had kicked off the train was the cook, but the outfit is in luck since Scipio had worked for a while posing as the famous Colonel Cyrus Jones and the Virginian quickly makes him the new cook.

During the remainder of the journey the focus is on the growing conflict between the Virginian and Trampas. The Virginian's final responsibility is to get the men back to the ranch; Trampas attempts to organize "a mutiny" and lead the cowpunchers to the new gold strike at Rawhide. The Virginian realizes that Trampas will not face him in open conflict so he devises a plan to make Trampas look foolish in front of all the men. In this way, they'll lose their faith in the troublemaker and his talk of gold. Near Rawhide the train takes its place behind several stalled trains which await repairs of the bridge ahead. Passengers from four "express" trains are wandering along the tracks as if they were walking on a city street. Indians from the Crow reservation had come by to sell food, of which there was a shortage. The whole scene takes on a carnival atmosphere. The Virginian orders Scipio to prepare a fire while he searches a nearby marsh for frogs. When Scipio begins to cook them he is besieged by passengers wanting to buy them. At this point the Virginian begins his gigantic fabrication about "frog" ranches and how much money they make. No one is more gullible than Trampas for he sees a frog ranch as a quick way to make money. The foreman leads his adversary on for a long time before he makes a fool of Trampas. Scipio hails the Virginian as "the king of the liars." His storytelling ability is recognized by Indian and passenger alike. The Virginian has once again outwitted Trampas and the mutiny has been quelled, but both Scipio and the narrator realize that the Trampas-Virginian conflict is far from over. After leaving the train, the Virginian and his men gather strays as they slowly move south to the ranch. The narrator also relates an incident of how the Virginian saves his life by shooting a rattlesnake which was creeping up behind him as he sat near a campfire.

Comment

Once again, almost as if someone behind the scenes were pulling strings, people show up at the most propitious moment. Not only does the narrator receive a much-needed train ride, but the Virginian acquires, in the person of Scipio Le Moyne, a replacement for his just-fired cook. Note that Scipio is none other than the spurious Colonel Cyrus Jones, last seen in Omaha.

One wonders how the Virginian would have handled the growing mutiny of his men, led by Trampas, if the train had not been stalled, and if the passengers had not been hungry and if there had not been a herd of frogs nearby. The Virginian always remains calm and confident but surely he did not foresee the remarkable combination of circumstances which he adroitly used to extricate himself from his predicament.

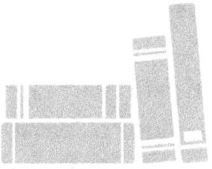

INTRODUCTION TO THE VIRGINIAN

TEXTUAL ANALYSIS

CHAPTERS 18-22

Shortly after the outfit arrives back at the ranch, the Judge appoints the Virginian foreman. It is also the time of the annual visit of Dr. Alexander MacBride, a traveling parson, whose week-long stay at the ranch is dreaded by everyone. Sight of his arrival sets the Virginian off on a long tirade about religion. He characterizes himself for the narrator: "I ain't religious. I know that. But I ain't un-religious. And I know that too." Part of the Virginian's tirade is at the expense of parsons in general. He resents their self-righteousness: "...a middlin' doctor is a pore thing, and a middlin' lawyer is a pore thing; but keep me from a middlin' man of God." The narrator shares his feelings as he comments, "I thought there should in truth be heavy damages for malpractice on human souls." The Virginian sums up his personal ideas about religion as he and the narrator ride along on the day the parson arrives:

> "As for salvation, I have got this far; somebody," he swept an arm at the sunset and the mountains, "must have made all that, I know. But I know one more thing

> I would tell Him to His face: if I can't do nothing long enough and good enough to earn eternal happiness, I can't do nothing long enough and bad enough to be damned. I reckon He plays a square game with us if He plays at all, and I ain't bothering my haid about other worlds."

At the time of Dr. MacBride's arrival Judge Henry and his wife are also entertaining the narrator, Miss Wood and Mr. and Mrs. Ogden, visitors from New York. Everyone finds the parson overbearing in his demands for human perfection. The Judge, usually an easygoing man, finds the parson intolerable: "He doesn't know what Christianity is yet.... The whole secret lies in the way you treat people. As soon as you treat men as your brothers, they are ready to acknowledge you - if you deserve it - as their superior. That's the whole bottom of Christianity, and that's what our missionary will never know."

One evening everyone gathers for the parson's annual service. The sermon is one in which he stresses to assembled guests and cowpunchers, "none of the sweet but all the bitter of his creed, naked and stern as iron." Back at the bunkhouse the cowboys show their open resentment of the parson's negative approach to life. During the sermon, the Virginian hits upon an excellent idea for a practical joke. He decides that by feigning salvation and repentance for a score of sins he never committed, he would beat the Parson at his own game by keeping the man up all night and hinting that he still had enough sins to need the Parson's help twenty-four hours a day. Losing one night of sleep is enough for the clergyman who quickly departs the next day. The Virginian is a hero to everyone but Molly, who finds his practical joke shocking. His appointment as foreman also causes an increase in the tension between himself and Trampas.

Comment

Dr. MacBride is a straw man, set up just to be knocked down. Many are the quite conventionally religious people who could no more abide Dr. MacBride's brand of sermonizing than could the Virginian or the narrator. Wister attempts to mitigate the harsh portrait he has painted by endowing Dr. MacBride with such traits as courage and resolution, but these attributes seem merely to be tacked on as an afterthought, and not part of his essential character.

The prank played on the Parson is not as clever or as humorous as those mentioned earlier in the book. The Virginian, for the first time, seems to act more out of vindictiveness than high spirits. There are many who will find his mocking a man getting religion not in the best taste.

The visit of the Ogdens arouses in Molly memories of the East and she decides to accompany them when they return. When she departs, the Virginian tells her that on her next trip to Vermont, "We both go together." Although Bennington greets her as it would a hero returning from the wars, she cannot drive the Virginian or Wyoming from her thoughts. She declines Sam Bannetts's proposal of marriage once again. When she discusses marriage with her great-aunt, the sage woman advises her: "So long as you can help it, never marry! But when you cannot help it a moment longer then listen to nothing but that; for my dear, I know your choice would be worthy of the Starks." When Molly shows her aunt the Virginian's picture the old woman says that he has a good face and when Molly leaves, the aunt concludes, despite all the obvious cultural barriers, "She is like us all. She wants a man that is a man." But upon her return to Bear Creek Molly is still unable to decide about marriage despite the Virginian's persistence.

Comment

The description of Molly's dissatisfaction with the East and her restlessness there must have stemmed from Wister's own feelings as a young man. The most compelling portions of the novel, the most deeply felt emotions expressed are not about people, certainly not individuals, but about the Old West as the youthful Wister remembered it. Thus, the real romance in The Virginian is not between Molly and her cowboy, but between Wister and his fondly recalled El Dorado.

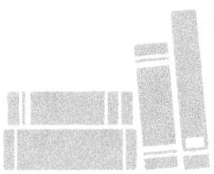

INTRODUCTION TO THE VIRGINIAN

TEXTUAL ANALYSIS

CHAPTERS 23-25

As winter sets in, it becomes impossible for the Virginian to visit Molly. He and Scipio, a man of great insight, become good friends. Shorty, a weak but kind cowpuncher, falls under the influence of Trampas despite the efforts of the Virginian to keep him honest. There is no doubt that Shorty and Trampas will leave the ranch in the spring. Even though the Virginian is given more administrative duties by the Judge, he finds time to read "Othello" and "Romeo and Juliet." Near the end of winter he writes Molly a letter stating his disappointment because he will not be able to visit her at the beginning of spring. The route of the letter reveals one of the peculiarities of the day:

> The letter, duly stamped and addressed to Bear Creek, set forth upon its travels; and these were devious and long. When it reached its destination, it was some twenty days old. It had gone by private hand at the outset, taken the stage-coach at a way point, become late in that stage-coach, reached a point of transfer,

and waited there for the postmaster to begin, continue, end, and recover from a game of poker, mingled with whiskey. Then it once more proceeded, was dropped at the right way point, and carried by private hand to Bear Creek. The experience of this letter, however, was not at all a remarkable one at that time in Wyoming.

The letter also cautions Molly not to worry about the Indians, since the reports of their activities are only kept alive by certain newspaper editors in order to keep the army in the ' territory. The Virginian feels that the editors have certain friends who get beef and hay contracts from the army.

The Virginian does not mention in his letter that the real reason for his delay is not the threat of Indians but rather the threat of rustlers whose activities "were growing bold." Spring afforded the cattle thieves a good opportunity for their activities because the winter had scattered the cattle widely over the range.

However, the Virginian is able to visit Molly for an hour one spring day. She had received his letter only the day before and perhaps because of the lonely winter she has just spent she is quite receptive to his affection. He brings her a horse to ride and as a goodbye gift gives her a bunch of flowers. In the next few weeks work occupies the Virginian's time, while Molly finds the days without him to be lonely ones.

Comment

The antediluvian conditions prevailing in the Territories is forcibly brought to our attention by the description of the tortuous route taken by the Virginian's letter to Molly. How different it is today: one can merely slip a letter into a mailbox and go off, secure in the feeling that there is better than an even chance that it will be delivered.

An important crisis is presaged by the mention of rustlers. Thus far we have had none of the violence usually associated with the Western novel. Now, however, crime, and in the West of that day, capital crime, enters the story. We do not know yet just how far Steve is involved in the rustling, but we have been given inklings that his doom is imminent.

The sparse use made of violence by Wister makes it, when it does come, all the more shocking. This may not have been mere showmanship on his part, however. Wister was setting down, as accurately and conscientiously as he could, his impressions and recollections of what the West was like, and of course, television notwithstanding, they didn't have gunplay every day.

In the spring, Trampas and Shorty left the ranch as the foreman had predicted. One day soon after visiting Molly, the Virginian is traveling to Balaam's ranch in order to get back two of the Judge's horses which Balaam had borrowed several weeks before, and on the way is overtaken by Shorty who accompanies him. Balaam has forgotten the date of the month since "Days look alike, and often lose their very names in the quiet depths of Cattle Land." In a conversation with Shorty, Balaam discovers that he is unemployed and in need of money. The horse trader makes Shorty an offer for his horse, Pedro. Shorty has trained his horse in many tricks; the talented horse responds to Shorty's kindness and training by obeying his master's every command to near perfection. There is little doubt that Balaam wants Shorty's horse. By clever depreciation of the horse's value and by convincing Shorty that the horse has a bad leg, Balaam dupes the misguided cowboy into parting with his prize possession for forty dollars, a Mexican blanket and a pair of spurs. Although the Virginian is a witness to this deception he obeys the custom of the land by looking on "silent and somber... He could scarcely interfere between another man and his own beast." Yet he knows that Shorty's wish to buy the horse back once he is able to be a futile one.

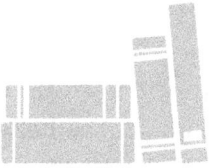

INTRODUCTION TO THE VIRGINIAN

TEXTUAL ANALYSIS

CHAPTERS 26-29

In order to apologize properly to the Judge for not returning his horses on time, Balaam decides to deliver them personally to the Sunk Creek Ranch. The Virginian did not look forward to traveling with Balaam because he vehemently opposes Balaam's maltreatment of horses. Balaam's cruelty to animals is so widely known in the territory that the cowboys often threaten a perverse animal with the statement "I'll Balaam you."

The two men set out the next morning with Monte, Pedro, the Judge's two horses, and Balaam's packhorse, an old mare bearing two day's food and lodging. It is not long before Balaam begins to abuse poor Pedro, the most obedient horse one could ask for. When the Virginian objects, Balaam states his attitude: "...the Western pony's man's enemy...you've got to keep them afraid of you..." Balaam beats Pedro at every opportunity and the Virginian's anger is slowly building up. After a severe beating, Pedro sinks to the ground from abuse and exhaustion. When Balaam attempts to maltreat the poor creature further, the Virginian steps in. In the ensuing fight Balaam is soundly beaten. The Virginian aids both the stricken horse and the stricken man. He fixes the mare for Balaam and ties a lead rope on Pedro.

Comment

Some of the most touching pages of the novel are those concerning Pedro. Although Shorty has only himself to blame for selling his pony, we can still be moved by his affecting farewell to his mount. Shorty is almost as innocent as Pedro and does not realize that in selling him, he is sealing the pony's doom.

Although, at the urging of Theodore Roosevelt, Wister deleted some of the details of Balaam's horrendous mistreatment of Pedro, the scene remains a shocking one. Once again, when Wister feels profoundly about something, his writing becomes inspired and the situation is made real to us.

A further touch of verisimilitude is the Virginian's reluctance to intervene in either the sale or the abuse of Pedro. Despite the fact that Balaam's actions are utterly repugnant to him, the Virginian takes a hand in things only when it becomes absolutely impossible for him to restrain himself. This is unlike the common misconception of the cowboy as exemplified by the Lone Ranger, who, having no living to make, rides the range, setting wrongs right.

While traveling over a difficult part of the trail, the Judge's two horses break free; a little later, Pedro breaks his leg on a rope trap set by the Indians. When this happens, Balaam realizes that the noises they have been hearing for the past hour have been made by Indians. With no concern for his fellow man,

Balaam deserts the Virginian and flees to safety. At a settler's cabin Balaam writes the Judge, telling of the Indian attack. He says he would like to come to Sunk Creek but because he is sick he would only be a burden. Of course, both statements are lies. When Balaam returns to his ranch, Shorty is waiting to buy back Pedro. Balaam tells him of the Indians' attack and the death of Pedro at their hands. Shorty is mournful at the loss of the horse to whom he was so close. When the Judge receives Balaam's letter, he orders a search for the Virginian.

Comment

So late an appearance of Indians must surely set a record in a novel of this sort. Of course, Wister knew that at that date most Indians were on reservations and but rarely wandered off. Perhaps Wister was being disingenuous, saving his Indians to be used as a means of bringing the romance between Molly and the Virginian to a climax.

Meanwhile, Molly has written the Virginian a letter saying she no longer wishes to see him. Although she knows she loves him, she feels she cannot marry beneath her station. Her feelings have been strongly influenced by her mother. On the other hand, Mrs. Taylor feels Molly has treated the Virginian poorly. When Molly decides to return to Vermont and she and Mrs. Taylor discuss the situation, Mrs. Taylor angrily compares the Virginian to a diamond, "Since the roughness looks bigger to you than the diamond, you had better go back to Vermont. I expect you'll find better grammar there, deary."

Upset by this womanly talk, Molly rides off into the mountains. In the Upper Canyon she discovers Monte, the Virginian's horse. Nearby she finds the unconscious cowboy, with one of his arms lying in a spring. Blood covers the back of his flannel shirt. She thinks he may be dead and then she notices that the blood is still running. Making the wounded man more comfortable, she cleans his wound and tears strips from her dress to bind him up. As he regains consciousness, he tells her to leave him because the Indians are still in the area and she is not safe. However, in the tradition of the earlier Starks, she will not desert this man. When she removes the handkerchief around his neck she realizes it is the one with flowers which she had lost during their first meeting at the swollen river. Molly slowly leads the wounded man to the safety of her cabin.

While Mr. Taylor goes for the doctor, the two women look after the Virginian. In his delirium, the Virginian mentions the incident with Trampas at the barbecue when that troublemaker had lied about Molly's reputation; he also speaks of his concern for his friend Steve. In the course of the next several weeks, Molly changes her mind about marriage, as she realizes that she could never love anyone else as much. The young couple spend long hours discussing life and literature. Toward the end of his illness, the Virginian writes Molly's mother in Bennington. The letter tells of Molly's heroism, his own background, expectations and love of Molly, and certain aspects of how their decision to marry came about:

> ...I had better tell you the way I know I love Miss Wood. I am not a boy now, and women are no new thing to me. A man like me who has traveled meets many of them as he goes and passes on but I stopped when I came to Miss Wood. That is three years but I have not gone on. What right has such as he? you will say. So did I say it after she had saved my life. It was hard to get to that point and keep there with her around all day. But I said to myself you have bothered

her for three years with your love and if you let your love bother her you don't love her like you should and you must quit for her sake who has saved your life. I did not know what I was going to do with my life after that but I supposed I could go somewhere and work hard and so Mrs. Wood I told her I would give her up. But she said no...

While Molly's mother and her circle in Bennington are quite distressed by this news, the approval of her great-aunt and Mrs. Taylor as well as the folks in the territory more than compensate the girl for her wise choice.

Comment

It is, of course, simple poetic justice that Molly should save the Virginian's life; turnabout is fair play. Such balancing of the books is not to be resisted by the ordinary novelist, least of all by Wister. Molly's final acceptance of the Virginian as her mate is not made easier for us to understand by our wondering what took her so long, but now we may be comforted that things are set.

The letter that the Virginian writes to Molly's mother is a good one, and we are quite as affected by it as is Molly's great-aunt. The simple eloquence of the almost unlettered cowboy is among Wister's best work in the novel. Here he shows us, as Thornton Wilder showed us later, that homely words, unpretentiously arranged, can go right to the heart, if they stem from the heart.

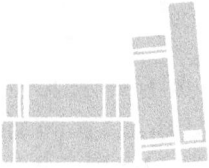

INTRODUCTION TO THE VIRGINIAN

TEXTUAL ANALYSIS

CHAPTERS 30-33

....

At this point in the story, the narrator once again returns from the "cities and smoke" of the East. He travels by horse through a black storm, which he calls an omen, to his rendezvous with the Virginian near Horse Thief Pass in the Teton Mountains of Eastern Idaho. The Easterner is no longer a tenderfoot as we can see from his skillful and solitary journey through the open country. In view of the foot-hills, the narrator notices a clump of cottonwoods shortly before he arrives at a dilapidated group of buildings. There are several horses there and the cowboys look at him with distrust; but the Virginian steps forward and certifies his friend. To the narrator's shock, the group is a posse which has apprehended two rustlers who will be hanged from the cottonwoods in the morning. While the visitor half expects the prisoners to be Trampas and pitiful Shorty whose names have been associated with rustling, his shock is doubled when he recognizes Steve, the man he met his first night in the West and the Virginian's friend. During that night and the following morning the Virginian does not speak to his old friend, but the other members of the posse keep up a constant banter hoping that Ed or Steve will disclose some other members of the gang. The narrator does not attend the dual hanging which is quickly accomplished following breakfast.

Comment

The lynching of the rustlers, while expected, is nonetheless shocking. The reader would have been more affected by it, however, if he had been permitted to get to know Steve. Merely telling us that Steve and the Virginian had been friends is not enough; we should have been allowed to see that friendship.

The gruesome all-night vigil before the hanging is briefly, but effectively, described. Here Wister is at his best; the scene is vivid and unforgettable.

It is not until the Virginian and the narrator are on the trail for a few hours that the cowboy begins to talk of the recent events. He relates how Ed and Steve faced their deaths; Ed became hysterical while Steve faced death stoically. This had increased the Virginian's respect for his friend. It is part of the code as the narrator tells us: "... his view was simple enough: you must die brave. Failure is a sort of treason to the brotherhood and forfeits pity. It was Steve's perfect bearing that had caught his heart so that he forgot even his scorn of the other man." As the talk continues, the Virginian tells of his association with Steve. Steve did not talk to him after he was caught, nor did he say goodbye to him as he had to the rest of the posse. But still he respects Steve for not informing on Shorty and for dying like a man. The Virginian "knew, knew passionately, that he had done right; but the silence of his old friend to him through those last hours left a sting that no reasoning could assuage." As they lose sight of the clump of cottonwoods, the talk turns to other matters and the tensions lessen, but the scene will probably always haunt both men.

During the next few days, the two men pick up the trail of the other rustlers. In order to escape on the only horse they have, Trampas shoots Shorty in the back. The Virginian and the Easterner discover Shorty's body and bury him. Although they follow the hoofprints of Trampas' horse, they lose the trail of the killer the next day near the area which later was known as Jackson's Hole, a notorious community of criminals. The author comments on the enigma of justice and society:

> **...the unknown rider of the horse knew well that he would find shelter and welcome among the felons of his stripe. Law and order might guess his name correctly, but there was no next step, for lack of evidence; and he would wait, whoever he was, until the rage of popular justice, which had been pursuing him and his brother thieves, should subside. Then, feeling his way gradually with prudence, he would let himself be seen again.**

We next see Trampas in the showdown duel with the Virginian near the end of the story.

Comment

The conversation between the Virginian and the narrator, as they journey from the scene of the lynching, is confused and erratic. This may be how real human beings would talk after such an experience, but it does little to clarify for us the state of their emotions.

In particular, the Virginian's defense of his part in the tragedy sounds hollow and unconvincing.

The description of Jackson's Hole (taken from reality) is sketchy, piquing our interest and making us wish the author had described it more fully.

The story now shifts to Molly who is distressed when her schoolchildren simulate the hanging in a schoolyard game and tell her about the Virginian's part in it. Although Mrs. Taylor tries to comfort her, it is not until the next day when she talks with Judge Henry that Molly feels better. The author discusses the involved problem of good and evil and its relation to law and society. He begins his thesis by stating that every good man has convictions about right and wrong, but one must not forget that "Many an act that man does is right or wrong according to the time and place which form...its context." His conclusion is that it is not enough to say of a man, "He did evil that good might come"; rather we must ask the primary question: "Was the thing that he did, in the first place, evil?" The Judge contrasts Southern lynching and lynching of cattle thieves. The basis of his argument is that the people have taken back their God-given rights to peace and order because the courts were not guaranteeing those rights. While we may call this primitive, he sums up, "far from being a defiance of the law, it is an assertion of it - the fundamental of self-governing men, upon whom the whole fabric is based." Agreeing with Molly that capital punishment, like war, is a terrible thing, he turns to an eternal hope and a stark reality: "perhaps someday we shall do without them. But they are none of them so terrible as unchecked theft and murder would be." The discussion helps Molly to view her Virginian in a favorable light.

Comment

The peculiar casuistry employed by Wister in defense of lynching, albeit only "certain" lynching, today would sound strange in the mouth of the veriest demagogue. It is not our purpose here to demolish Wister's arguments; their flimsiness is such that they dissolve at the merest touch of sunlight. The matter is gone into at such length that it is not clear whether the Judge is attempting to convince Molly or Wister is trying to convince the reader that vigilante justice is not abhorrent.

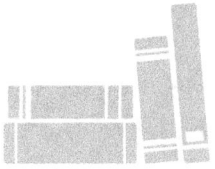

INTRODUCTION TO THE VIRGINIAN

TEXTUAL ANALYSIS

CHAPTERS 34-36

Molly and the Virginian set July 3rd as their wedding day and Molly decides to be married in Wyoming rather than Vermont. Her decision is based on the facts that the Cattle Land is where they met, courted and soon would live and raise their children. The Virginian gives Molly an engagement ring which contains both their birthstones united in one setting. When the couple arrive in town for their wedding, the irritating situation for which the Virginian has been prepared for five years-an eventual showdown with Trampas-is about to take place. After leaving Molly at the hotel the Virginian joins Scipio, Lin McLean and Honey Wiggins at the saloon. They all offer to handle Trampas who has been hanging around town telling a version of the Teton Mountain story which relates that the Virginian killed Shorty. Naturally the hero declines their help.

When Trampas comes into the saloon violence nearly erupts, but Trampas is restrained. Angrily he speaks the lines which are to determine his fate: "'Your friends have saved your life,' he rang out, with obscene epithets. 'I'll give you till sun-down to leave town'." Even after this challenge, the Virginian tries to avoid a showdown but Trampas' lies continue to force the situation as he sneers to the bystanders," He has been dodging it five years," and even throws a bottle at the Virginian. The time is set; the showdown will occur at sunset.

Comment

Typically, the issue between Trampas and the Virginian is never made clear. Why this blustering, cowardly rustler should persist, lemming-like, to rush toward his doom by badgering and insulting the Virginian is a mystery which Wister does not solve for us. It is easier for us to understand if we remember that, just as the Virginian is not real, but the embodiment of Good in the West, so is Trampas the incarnation of Evil in the West. And, since this is fiction, Good will triumph.

The Virginian decides not to tell Molly, but she learns anyway; she implores him to come away with her, but such lack of courage is not part of the Virginian's code. Even her threat not to marry him will not make him abstain from the duel. Trampas, too, is having anxious moments while he awaits the time. As he is drinking with his friends he thinks he sees Shorty's ghost. A few moments after sunset the men face each other in the street and Trampas is killed by two of the Virginian's bullets. Molly is so happy that her lover is alive that she does not even remember her threat.

Comment

The description of the actual showdown is a masterpiece of understatement. No fanfares are employed by the author before the shooting, and no dead marches or huzzas are rung in after it is over. The relating of the event is accomplished as coolly as was the event itself.

The bride and bridegroom spend their honeymoon high in the mountains and then visit Bennington, where the Virginian soon learns to hold his own, and Dunbarton, where the great-aunt and her new nephew become boon companions. When the couple return to Wyoming, the Virginian becomes Judge Henry's partner. Not long after this, coal deposits on some of his property are in great demand by the railroad. The cowboy's ability to change with the times is the key to his success and Molly and he live very comfortably with their many children.

Comment

The Virginian's bucolic island retreat is curiously evocative of Mark Twain's *Jackson's Island*. Here a man can escape the pressures and cares of civilization. Here there are no machines, either industrial or political, to cast their soot upon one. Here a man can live only for himself and be himself without let or hindrance. This is indeed the life. Or, is it a kind of death?

The winding-up of affairs and pairing off of couples is in the tradition of novels of this era. There are no loose ends, everyone is accounted for and the numerous progeny forecast for the happy couple more than compensate us for the demise of Molly's great-aunt.

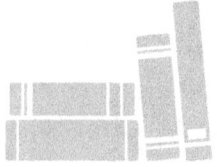

INTRODUCTION TO THE VIRGINIAN

CHARACTER ANALYSES

THE VIRGINIAN

The hero of the novel, this young cowboy, serves as a symbol of the West. The author gives his readers a limited amount of biographical information concerning this character but he does not give them all the characteristics one would desire in a horseman of the plains. We never learn his real name, but the Virginian himself tells us (in his letter to Molly's mother) something of his background. He is of Virginia English and Scotch-Irish background, from a family of simple hunters and farmers who have not risen socially in the world. He tells Mrs. Wood of the battlefield experience of his ancestors and also explains that there is a tendency in his family for one son to leave home. In his generation, the Virginian was the runaway son. Earlier in the story the narrator discloses that the Virginian's departure took place at the age of fourteen and that, at the opening of the novel, he is twenty-four.

The description of the Virginian's physical features helps to create the image of the hero. He is a "slim, young giant" who fairly radiates youth and strength. His hair is very black, which the narrator interprets as a symbol of his joking devilish nature. The physical prowess of the Virginian is undeniable - he is supremely confident and successful in feats of a physical nature, always outdoing his fellows in riding, roping and in enduring in wild country.

This masculine perfection of the Virginian is balanced, in Wister's portrayal, by his gentleness and sentimentality. His treatment of Molly is tender and his sentimentality is depicted at several points. The story of his choosing of Molly's engagement ring is one example. Others include his keeping Molly's handkerchief as a memento, his choosing of the island spot for their honeymoon and his feelings about their wedding ring which he wears on a chain around his neck prior to the ceremony.

Wister uses his hero to portray the romance which he found in the West. The Virginian's character traits - honesty, religion without piety, strength, intelligence, courage, chivalry, morality - are those which the author sees in America's last romantic figure, the cowboy. The Virginian stands as a symbol of all of these men, whose freedom of spirit and love of adventure caught Wister's imagination and ultimately made him famous.

MOLLY STARK WOOD

Wister gives his heroine an impressive family which provides a method by which to contrast Eastern and Western social values. Molly is the descendant of the Revolutionary War hero, General John Stark, and, as such, she and her family rank high in Bennington's social scale. This rank is lowered somewhat in Molly's late teens when the family suffers financial reverses and Molly begins to support herself. Although the occupations she undertakes (handkerchief embroidery, making preserves, and teaching music) are very ladylike, the more staid members of Bennington's social set find fault with her. Her refusal of Sam Bannett as a suitor arouses their scorn. He is an up-and-coming young businessman whose family background is not known - but, in the eyes of Bennington's upper crust, he is good enough for a girl who sells embroidery and preserves for a living.

Molly's rejection of Bennington's social values is first seen in her refusal of the invitations to join the various commemorative societies to which her ancestry entitles her. As the pressure grows for her to marry Sam Bannett she becomes less and less enchanted with her Eastern life and ultimately accepts the invitation to teach in Bear Creek in Wyoming. She is encouraged in this venture by her great-aunt who sympathizes with Molly's feelings.

Wister finds a saving grace in Molly's ancestry; it is responsible for the pluck and resourcefulness which enable her to endure her family's financial troubles and to succeed in her new Western career. Wister implies that Molly comes by these traits through her famous ancestors who also exhibited them in large measure.

The author makes many literary uses of the character of Molly. She and her family provide the vehicle for contrast between the East and the West. Molly's inexperience and misunderstanding of Western values allow the author to explain these in some detail to his readers. Finally, she, like the hero, serves as a symbol of "good." She is the pure young girl who is truly worthy of the love of a man such as the Virginian. All her characteristics combine to make her what Wister calls a "New Woman."

TRAMPAS

This cowboy character serves as Wister's symbol of moral evil. He is the Virginian's major adversary and the story of their conflict provides much of the dramatic action in the novel. The Virginian is always successful in his clashes with Trampas but it is necessary to remember that the hero is superior in every way to his enemy. At the beginning of the story Trampas is a troublemaker who insults the Virginian, but his character deteriorates as the story progresses. He becomes a cattle rustler and finally a killer. The Virginian kills Trampas in their final showdown which he has virtuously tried to avoid.

Wister uses Trampas as a means of contrast between Western concepts of moral good and evil. Against the Virginian's faithful adherence to the cowboy "code," Trampas is the proverbial "bad guy" who breaks all the rules and is ultimately punished for his wrongdoing.

STEVE

A friend of the Virginian's, this character provides the hero with a dilemma. He becomes a cattle rustler and is caught by the posse of which the Virginian is a member. Before he is hanged, he converses with all of the members of the posse by the Virginian. While the hero is sure he is doing the right thing, Steve's refusal to speak to him causes him great uneasiness. Despite Steve's outlawry, the Virginian continues to admire him because of his stoic acceptance of death. The situation points up the dilemma of loyalty to law and duty as opposed to loyalty to love and personal feeling.

JUDGE HENRY

This man is the Virginian's employer and the narrator's host. He admires the main character and makes him foreman of the ranch, and, at the end of the novel, asks the Virginian to become his partner. Wister uses this character to explain the relationships among law, order, and society in the West when Molly puzzles over the moral problems of lynching in the West.

SHORTY

This cowboy character does not do much thinking for himself. He is essentially good but misguided and despite the Virginian's efforts to save him he becomes a fellow rustler to Trampas. He is killed by Trampas when they are trying to escape the posse. This character is also duped by a horse trader-Balaam-into selling his prize horse Pedro. Shorty's redeeming quality is his kindness to animals. Wister often compares him to "a lost dog."

BALAAM

Wister uses Balaam as another symbol of evil. This man is a maltreater of animals and his actions cause him to come into conflict with the Virginian. In their fight, the Virginian's physical prowess overwhelms Balaam. In addition to being cruel to animals this character is also a liar and a coward. He deserts the Virginian in the face of an Indian attack and then lies about the event to the Judge.

SCIPIO

Scipio's name derives from the custom in his family to name the oldest boy after the great Roman. Scipio is a wanderer, promoter and opportunist on the one hand and a keen observer, philosopher of the homespun variety and loyal friend on the other. Scipio helps to point up the growing feud between the Virginian and Trampas. Typical of the paradox in Scipio's character is the narrator's description of him:

> **...for Scipio's twenty odd years were indeed a library of life. I have never met a better heart, a shrewder wit, and looser morals, with yet a native sense of decency and duty somewhere hard and fast enshrined.**

A good example of his wit is shown when he describes Shorty's falling under the influence of Trampas: "When a man ain't got no ideas of his own...he'd ought to be kind o' careful who he borrows 'em from."

INTRODUCTION TO THE VIRGINIAN

COMMENTARY

The Virginian must be considered in one sense an autobiographical work. The character of the narrator provides the possibility for this conclusion. Like Wister, he is a well-bred Easterner who visits in the "wild West" and is enthralled with what he finds. He returns time and again to this novel land whose vast wildness and airy beauty he so sincerely appreciates. Wister too returned more than once to the West whose scribe he was to become. This autobiographical facet of the novel is due in large measure, no doubt, to Wister's heavy reliance upon the journals and diaries of his Western trips not only for geographical descriptions, but also for the character descriptions which he sets forth.

When the author has his hero tell the following anecdote as the narrator is leaving Wyoming, he is surely expressing his own feelings:

> The Virginian had touched the whole thing the day I left him. He had noticed me looking a sort of farewell at the plains and mountains. "You will come back to it," he said. "If there was a headstone for every man that once pleasured in his freedom here, yu'd see

one 'most every time yu' turned his head. It's a heap sadder than a graveyard - but yu' love it all the same."

THE VIRGINIAN AS SOCIAL HISTORY

As Wister tells us in his introduction to *The Virginian*, because it attempts to describe "a day and a generation," it is, of necessity, historical. In *The Virginian* Wister has given us a social picture of the West in the late 19th century in the same way that F. Scott Fitzgerald gave us a social picture of the East in the "Roaring Twenties," a few years later. Both authors portray the social manners and mores of the generation with which they deal.

The Virginian is significant because it was one of the first works of its kind - the first to give a somewhat accurate if romanticized picture of post-Civil War Western America. The discussions concerning the concepts of equality, social standards and law and justice reveal the fundamental philosophy which directed society at that time and place. Here we can see the origins of Western populism which affects American politics even today. It is not difficult to see how Wister earned the title "father of the Western." The image of the tall, good cowboy, moral but not pious, intelligent but not "larned," who faces his adversary in a duel and follows the "code" of the West, began with this book.

MORAL VALUES IN THE VIRGINIAN

Wister depicts the moral values of the "wild West" through the use of characterization and contrast. The hero represents the moral Western man; his adversaries (e.g. Trampas and Balaam) represent the immoral. Molly, because she is an Easterner and doesn't understand, provides the author the means through which he can explain the Western moral code in more detail to his readers. This approach is utilized many times in the novel, for instance, when Molly experiences confusion over the Virginian's role in the hanging of Steve, and when she cannot understand what compels the Virginian to face his "showdown" with Trampas. In the first case, Wister has the Judge explain the relationships among law and order and society in the West. In this land, where the courts and the ordinary avenues of justice are not functioning properly because they are beyond the pale of civilization, the people must legislate as well as execute the law, lest there be no law at all. This is justifiable because it is from the people that the law arises in the first place. The Judge and Molly agree that the situation is not all they would like it to be, but it is necessary to protect society from its own less savory members.

In the second case, the author has the Virginian attempt to explain his own actions to Molly. The explanation involves the concepts of "honor" and "courage." Molly cannot grasp why the Virginian must defend his honor against the slander of Trampas; nor does she see that in running away the Virginian would display a lack of courage. She feels he is merely acting according to public opinion. He explains that to be a man it is necessary to keep one's integrity and honesty. This cannot be done if a man allows base slander against him to go unpunished. In fact, to do so is cowardly, according to the cowboy's code. It means that a man hasn't got the courage to defend his own name.

SOCIAL VALUES IN THE VIRGINIAN

Western social values are portrayed in the contrast between Eastern and Western characters. The character of Molly offers the author the opportunity to poke fun at the staid Eastern standard which considers parentage rather than achievement in judging a person's value. By contrast, the Western social criteria revolve around merit and ability. This is apparent in the Virginian's discussion of equality: "...a man has got to prove himself my equal before I'll believe him." His standard is action or achievement and no amount of the "right blood" running through one's veins will convince him of a person's value. As a man of action, he gauges all other men by the same standard.

When Molly returns to Bennington with her new husband, Wister again makes the contrast. Although the town's people are somewhat won over by the "cowboy" many of them still have strong reservations and feel sorry for Molly. It is evident that they have already judged him, not on the basis of what he has achieved, but on the basis of his social status. By contrast, the great-aunt is placed in a favorable light because she endeavors to discover the young man's interests and abilities rather than his mother's maiden name.

CHARACTERIZATION IN THE VIRGINIAN

Wister's character portrayal is one of the work's weaker points. The men and women who people the tale appear flat - the reader wants to get closer to them. Part of the reason for this is the dialogue. The Virginian is portrayed as a Southerner and the attempt is made to give his speech a regional accent. But the construction of the sentences he speaks is often so elegant and so educated that **realism** suffers. One example of this is the lack of the use of contractions. Especially in his conversations with Molly, the Virginian's speech is far more formal than seems likely.

Another cause for the flatness of the characters is the stark contrast of moral codes. The "good guys" are all good; and the "bad guys" are all bad. At times this appears to come close to the point of allegory, with the Virginian becoming the personification of the eternal "Good," and Trampas and Balaam the personifications of "Evil." In this respect, Shorty is an exceptional character - one in whom the reader finds the normal human blend of good and evil.

REALISM AND IDEALISM

Wister balances his idealistic portrayal of the main character with realism in his physical descriptions of the West. While he extols the beauty to be found there, he also gives a detailed picture of its more dismal characteristics. His description of the harsh setting of Medicine Bow is one example of his use of realism. Another is his portrayal of Balaam's maltreatment of animals. These details of the seamier side of Western life prevent the novel from becoming overly sentimental and allow the reader to become more involved in the story.

If you envision, after you have finished the story, the image of a brave, resourceful, chivalrous and honorable man when you think of a "horseman of the plains," then Owen Wister has succeeded in his purpose in writing the novel.

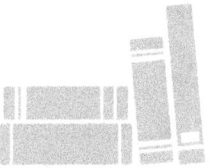

THE VIRGINIAN

SURVEY OF CRITICISM

The Virginian was an instant success when it was published in 1902 It received many favorable reviews. *The Philadelphia Times* reviewer stated: "The story is human and alive. It has the 'touch and go' of the vibrating life of the expansive American West..." "There is not a page in Mr. Wister's new book which is not interesting. This is its first great merit, that it arouses the sympathy of the reader and holds him absorbed to the end" is the essence of the review which appeared in *The New York Herald Tribune.* Perhaps the reviewer for *the Chicago American* was the most prophetic: "...he has put forth a book that will be remembered and read with interest many years hence." By 1908 *The Virginian* had exhibited its great popularity by selling over a million and a half copies.

EARLY CRITICISM

Other than book reviewers, one of the first critics to comment on the novel was Horace Fiske in his work, *Provincial Types In American Fiction* (1903), published one year after *The Virginian*.

Mr. Fiske sees *The Virginian* as the portrayal of "a unique and vanishing type of American provincial life." The result is that "one gets that sense of freedom and largeness, of nobility and wholesomeness, of being close to mother earth and also to the star-sown sky of true romance, which, after all is the highest effect of great art." He concludes that the success of the story is due to the realistic portrayal of the hero and to the setting. Quoting a critical comment made about Tom Jones, Fiske says of *The Virginian*, "This is not a book, but a man." While few would say this about the novel today, we must remember the genteel tradition of literature and criticism of the early twentieth century.

KING OF THE HORSE OPERAS

While one does not find much negative criticism on *The Virginian*, the majority of standard critical works on American literature credit Wister with being the first to use many of the techniques which have become a standard part of the Western tale. Van Wyck Brooks called the novel "the model for a thousand horse-operas and stories." Certainly that number is the minimum figure. Brooks also comments that the novel's chief weakness is its lack of authenticity. In grouping the characteristics of the romantic code of the horseman of the plains, the critic cites chivalry, the ability to live game and to die game, facing death as one would face losing at cards, and doing everything well, including sin. As the action of most Western stories is limited we find the same stock characters peopling them all. Among these are the good young cowboy, his crafty opponent and the pretty young Eastern lady. The rest of the cast is drawn from Indians, cowboys, stage drivers, sheriffs, bartenders, saloon ladies, prospectors, etc. Finally Brooks, like Fiske, places the novel in the general type which laments a vanishing era.

TWO RECENT CRITICS

In his introduction to the novel (1964), M. L Howe lists the attributes of the novel as an exciting plot with a tremendous climax, and the historical background. Sidney C. Clark's introduction (1964) credits Wister with drawing a moral cowboy but one who is also human. Mr. Clark also discusses the practical philosophy, epigrammatic style, and psychological insights in the novel. Both critics make Wister the Adam of the Western story.

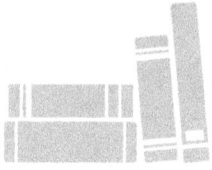

INTRODUCTION TO THE VIRGINIAN

ESSAY QUESTIONS AND ANSWERS

Question: What period of time does the novel cover?

Answer: Although Wister states in his introduction that the novel covers the years from 1874–1890 in Wyoming, we learn at the end of the story that it lasted for five years. These five years begin with the entrance of the narrator on the Western scene and end with the final showdown between Trampas and the Virginian. This fact is revealed through Trampas' reference to his five-year quarrel with the Virginian which had its origin in his card-game remark of Chapter 2.

Question: In his introduction, Wister refers to the novel as "an expression of American faith." Using the contents of the work can you explain what he means by this?

Answer: This remark finds its origin in Wister's discussion of quality and equality in America. He explains that by abolishing the traditional form of aristocracy through ancestry and providing every individual with "equal liberty to find his own level" the framers of the Declaration of Independence and the

Constitution had established true aristocracy. A true aristocracy is created by allowing "the best," or those who merit it most, to have positions of power. And true aristocracy and true democracy are identical - for each insists that the best man win. The "faith" of which Wister speaks is faith in the idea that the best will rise to the top, that the people, each of whom has an equal right to aid in making the choice, will choose those who are the "best," those who merit positions of power.

Question: What is the point of view in *The Virginian*?

Answer: The author of The Virginian tells his story largely through the use of a narrator who becomes directly involved in the events of the plot. The narrator is an Eastern gentleman who goes West to visit his friend Judge Henry. The first impressions the reader receives come through the eyes of the narrator who speaks in the first person. The author transmits judgments concerning the events of the story through the narrator who does not remain an impartial observer. He becomes very friendly with the Virginian and identifies with the "good" characters of the novel.

Woven into the book is the secondary plot of the narrator's rise from being a tenderfoot to his status as a seasoned Westerner.

Wister also enters the story directly as author to accomplish certain ends. He uses this technique when he is **foreshadowing** the future or emphasizing a moral and also to give the reader a deeper view of the events of the plot. Two examples of this are his discussion of "equality" and "democracy" in the middle of the novel and his discussion of "justice" and "capital punishment" at the end of the novel.

Question: Give some examples of Wister's use of **allusion** in *The Virginian*.

Answer: Wister uses four main types of allusions: Classical, Biblical, historical and literary. One example of a classical **allusion** is the naming of the character "Scipio Le Moyne" after a famous Roman general. This use of **allusion** is humorous since Scipio is an imaginative opportunist who becomes the cook for the Sunk Creek outfit. But, as we see, he is also a homespun philosopher about whom the narrator says: "His twenty odd years were indeed a library of life."

One of Wister's Biblical **allusions** is the character Balaam, who, like his Biblical namesake, is a maltreater of animals.

Wister's historical **allusions** center around Molly Stark Wood, whose name indicates her ancestry. As the descendant of a Revolutionary War hero, she is eligible to join countless New England societies whose entrance requirements are based on blood rather than merit. These **allusions** afford Wister his opportunity to contrast Eastern and Western social values. What you are, not who you are, is the important thing to Wister.

The author also uses literary **allusions** to create humorous situations in the plot. These occur when the Virginian decides to become "educated" and starts to read Molly's books. His - analogies of Western life to nineteenth century and other English literature provide an excellent vehicle for humor.

Question: What is the structure of *The Virginian*?

Answer: The structure of Wister's novel is somewhat episodic with several chapters being stories in themselves. This is no doubt due to the fact that the author published parts of the novel in short story form prior to the publication of the entire work.

Wister unites the novel into an integral whole by his characters and his flashback technique. The character of the hero provides a thread which unites the **episodes** of the novel to give it satisfactory integrity. He uses flashback to bring the reader up to date on the characters who were not present in intervening episodes.

Question: What use does Wister make of the characters of Trampas and Molly's family?

Answer: In the novel Trampas represents moral evil. He is the troublemaker who from the beginning is at odds with the Virginian. The story of their conflict is the story of the conflict of good and evil. Trampas provides the contrast against which Wister can portray the moral code of the Virginian. Of course, the odds are always against him since he is inferior to the Virginian in looks, brains, wit and ability.

The author uses Molly's family as a vehicle by which he can explain the Western system of social values. Their criteria of judgment are contrasted with those of the Western folk to give an - idea of this aspect of Western life. While Molly has rejected the Eastern standard by not joining the organizations to which her ancestry entitled her to membership, she is long troubled by the social and cultural differences between the Virginian and herself. Not until she realizes that she will never love anyone else as much can she accept him fully. Her family, who still cling to the traditional standard of ancestry, have great difficulty in accepting the Virginian and feel uncomfortable in his presence.

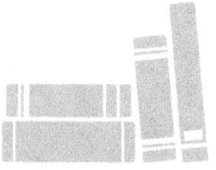

BIBLIOGRAPHY

There are many paperback editions of *The Virginian* available today. The ones listed in this bibliography are cited for some special critical or textual reason. Most of Owen Wister's other works are no longer in print but they can usually be found in the library. Biographical material can be found in the standard sources; among the better ones are Stanley J. Kunitz and Howard Haycraft's *Twentieth Century Authors* (1942) and Frank N. Magill's *Cyclopedia of World Authors* (1958). Criticism about Wister can be found in general surveys on the literature of the American West. Recent criticism, however, is sparse. The reason for this is obvious; most of what can be said about the man and his work has already been said. The publication of his Western travel journals in 1958 has caused a few contemporary critical articles and these are cited below. There is little doubt that one of the many biographical series now being published on American authors will include a volume on Wister in the near future.

Boatright, Mody C. "The American Myth Rides the Range: Owen Wister's Man on Horseback," *Southwest Review*, XXXVI (Summer, 1951), 157–163.

Bode, Carl. "Henry James and Owen Wister," *American Literature*, XXVI (May, 1954), 250–252.

Boynton, H. W. "A Word on the Genteel Critic: Owen Wister's Quack Novels and Democracy," *Dial*, LIX (1915), 303–306.

Brooks, Van Wyck and Bettmann, Otto. *Our Literary Heritage: A Pictorial History of the Writer in America*. New York: E. P. Dutton Co., 1956, 210–211. A brief article entitled "Saving the Cowboy from Oblivion"; includes an illustration from *The Virginian*, a portrait of Owen Wister and a full page picture of Theodore Roosevelt high above the Yosemite Valley, California.

Bratcher, James T. "Owen Wister's *The Virginian*: Two Corrections," *Western Folklore*, XXI (1962), 188–190.

Fiske, Horace Spencer. *Provincial Types in American Fiction*. Chautauqua, N.Y.: Chautauqua Press, 1907, 215–240. One of the earliest detailed studies of the novel.

Hasley, Louis. "American Literature of the Westward Movement," *College English*, XXVI (November, 1964), 154–156. This article discusses a course in American Literature of the Western Movement which Mr. Hasley has offered at the University of Notre Dame. The sections of the course follow the Western movement: Seaboard and Piedmont, Over the Appalachians, The Old Southwest and Twain, The Great Plains etc. In the latter section *The Virginian* is listed with other American Western classics as Clark's *The Ox-Bow Incident* and Schaefer's *Shane*.

Hubbell, Jay B. "Owen Wister's Work," *South Atlantic Quarterly*, XXIX (1930), 440–443.

Kemble, Frances Ann. *Records of a Girlhood*. New York: Henry Holt, 1879. Wister's family background.

———. *Records of Later Life*. New York: Henry Holt, 1882. Wister's family background.

Lewis, Marvin. "Owen Wister: Caste Imprints in Western Letters," *Arizona Quarterly*, X (Summer, 1954), 147-156.

Marsh, E. C. "Representative American Story Tellers: Owen Wister," *Bookman*, XXVII (1908), 456-458.

Rourke, Constance. *American Humor: A Study of the National Character.* New York: Doubleday, 1953. A standard work on the humor of the nineteenth century American West, this study was first published in 1931.

Smith, Henry Nash. *Virgin Land: The American West As Symbol and Myth.* New York: Vintage Books, 1958. A critical study of the fiction of the American West.

Walker, Don D. "Wister, Roosevelt and James: A Note on the Western," *American Quarterly*, XII:3 (Fall, 1960), 358-366. The story behind Wister's omission of certain realistic details in *The Virginian*. Wister's tendency toward melodrama rather than **realism** was influenced by Theodore Roosevelt, William Dean Howells, and Henry James.

Watkins, George T. *Owen Wister and the American West: A Bibliography and Critical Study.* (unpublished Ph.D. dissertation, Department of English, University of Illinois, 1959). Synopsis in Dissertation Abstracts, Vol. 20, #1772, 1959.

Wister, Fanny Kemble. "Owen Wister's West," *Atlantic Monthly*, CXCV (May, 1955), 29-35; (June, 1955), 52-57.

_____, ed. *Owen Wister Out West: His Journals and Letters.* Chicago: University of Chicago Press, 1958. Written by Owen Wister's daughter, this book includes a biography, reminiscences and Wister's journals of his travels in the West from 1885-1895. A mandatory work for critics and serious readers of Wister.

Wister, Owen. *The Virginian.* New York: Washington Square Press, 1964. Part of Washington Square Press' "Reader's Enrichment Series," this particular edition has benefited from the work of a large and professional editorial board. A Reader's Supplement featuring writing and vocabulary exercises follows the text.

———. *The Virginian.* Abridged and with an Introduction by M. L. Howe. New York: Dell Publishing Co., 1964. For the reader who seeks an abbreviated version of the work as well as a modernization of some episodes and the Victorian formality of the original novel, this edition is one of the best.

———. *The Virginian.* Introduction by Sidney C. Clark; New York: Airmont Publishing Co., 1964. Mr. Clark's introduction is a concise and accurate statement concerning the popularity of the novel.

SELECTED WRITINGS OF OWEN WISTER

Fiction of the West

Red Men and White, 1896.
Lin McLean, 1898.
The Jimmyjohn Boss and Other Stories, 1900.
The Virginian, 1902.
A Journey in Search of Christmas, 1904.
Members of the Family, 1911.
Padre Ignacio, 1911.
When West Was West, 1928.

Miscellaneous Fiction

The New Swiss Family Robinson, 1882.
The Dragon of Wontley, 1892.
Lady Baltimore, 1900.

Philosophy 4, 1903.
How Doth the Simple Spelling Bee, 1907.
Mother, 1907.

Biography

Ulysses S. Grant, 1900.
The Seven Ages of Washington, 1907.
Roosevelt, The Story of a Friendship, 1930.

Non-Fiction

The Pentecost of Calamity, 1915.
A Straight Deal; or, The Ancient Grudge, 1920.
Neighbors Henceforth, 1922.

www.ingramcontent.com/pod-product-compliance
Lightning Source LLC
LaVergne TN
LVHW011727060526
838200LV00051B/3055